BEYOND THE PALM TREES
HENRY MAURIE LASSIE

Published by the CreateSpace Independent Publishing
Platform, USA

ISBN: 1505458986
ISBN 13: 9781505458985

Published by the CreateSpace Independent Publishing Platform, USA

This book is dedicated to my most beloved paternal grandmother, Andrea (Andie) Tarawallie, for her tender loving care during the first four years of my childhood; my most admired maternal grandmother, Mamako Sowo Abu, for her talented traditional story-telling skills which in part, inspired me to write this book; my late parents, Darmain Lassie Tarawallie and Keima Abu, for their determination to send me to school as the first son in the wider extended family; and my late junior brother, Moses Gibao Lassie, who was abducted and brutally murdered in July 1996 at the prime age of 38, by rebels during the civil conflicts in Liberia and Sierra Leone respectively.

"May the Souls of the Faithful Departed through the Mercy of God (Allah), Rest in Perfect Peace." Ameen!!(Amen!!)

ACKNOWLEDGEMENTS

I wish to acknowledge the invaluable contributions made by the Create Space Editors in the USA for their professional guidance and assistance in editing the manuscript of my story without which this book would not have been published.

My special thanks and appreciation go to Mrs Jan Richards of the Institute of Japanese Studies at the Cardiff Business School, Cardiff University, for her courage in typing the initial manuscript of this book. I also wish to extend my sincere gratitude to my former academic supervisor and director of Sir David Owen Population Centre, Mr Hamish Richards, for his advise and constructive criticisms regarding the initial structure of my manuscript. My sincere thanks also go to Mr Matthew Harka Quinn, for his computer expertise to save most of the files requested by the editors. And finally, my sincere gratitude goes to the British Council under whose scholarship I was able to come to the United Kingdom for further studies prior to the brutal civil conflicts in Liberia.

AUTHOR'S NOTES

Beyond the Palm Trees begins with the historic arrival of American free black slaves at what was once known as the 'Grain Coast' and is now called Liberia. It illustrates how the acquisition of land began in the country and the establishment of the Oil Palm Plantations Company, the first and largest plantation in Liberia.

Beyond the Palm Trees tells the story of a young man from the country-side whose primary ambition—to marry and live a normal family life is derailed by a series of unfortunate events, including catching his newly wedded wife in bed with another man. Later, he marries another woman who produces two, fine sons. Due to his frequent and prolonged absences from his village because of work, however, the young man one day returns home and finds his wife heavily pregnant by another man. What happens next is up to the reader to discover.

This story does not reflect the true images of actual people who may still bear the actual names of its main characters: there's no entity known as the "Oil Palm Plantations Company" in Liberia; and although there are villages named Nyandemoh-Lahun in Lofa County, Dar-Es-Salaam in Grand Capemount County, and Gbakokoyata in Bong County, there is no settlement in Liberia known as "Lopolu or Freeman Town." References made of Gardnersville, Bardnersville; Charlesville and other settlements are purely an illustration of fictional dimensions and have nothing to do with the reality of the present-day geopolitical divisions of Liberia.

PROLOGUE

The boat *arrived on January 7, 1822, under the cover of darkness, and it anchored at a small territory known to the settlers as the Grain* Coast.

As *dawn began with its protruding radiance of sparkling sunlight over the Atlantic coast, the first arrivals of free black slaves from North America knew for certain that a new dawn of freedom had begun and that they had at last found their* new promised land *in West Africa.*

As the boat anchored at its intended destination, the captain spotted a tall cotton tree in the middle of a tiny island; the rest of the occupants became apprehensive when they realized that there were no other human inhabitants to be seen.

Rumors of cannibalism in Africa brought great fear to the settlers, who had already lost many comrades to malaria during their brief settlement on a similar island in neighboring Sierra Leone. The freed slaves were equally wary of inevitable hostilities with the natives on the mainland.

In the midst of these uncertainties, the preacher who had traveled with the emancipated slaves got out of the boat, knelt down, and thrice kissed the ground. He then made the sign of the cross and raised both hands heavenward. He offered fervent prayers for their safe arrival and for God's divine protection in their new home in West Africa.

And as the sun rose that morning, the natives on the mainland spotted what they perceived to be a piece of banana leaf raised high and flying above one of the cotton trees in the middle of the tiny island. This was the symbolic flag of freedom erected by the newcomers to exemplify their new land of freedom in Africa.

The tiny island had been sacred for centuries to the natives who had, until then, preserved it as an inviolable place of worship; they came there at least once a year after their rice harvest to venerate their ancestors. The annual ancestor veneration specifically took place beneath a tall palm tree that stood in the middle of the island surrounded by a column of cotton trees.

Strange events often trigger curiosity. The natives, who had closely followed the events on shore from the mainland that morning, were uneasy about the presence of unfamiliar faces—especially a boat with cannons pointed at their doorstep. Their chief, who was also puzzled about these circumstances, saw fit to order two of his bravest fishermen to find out what was afoot. As the two men approached the tiny island in an even tinier canoe, they were greeted by cannon fire, followed by a hail of warning gunshots fired from the boat by the new settlers.

The two men jumped into the river in the ensuing pandemonium to swim for their lives. As they came ashore, they informed their ruler of the presence of strange-looking men and women who had now desecrated their once-sacred place of ancestor veneration.

The event soon alerted the native population on the mainland of an imminent danger. As the town crier relayed the news of the event on the mainland, a large group of people assembled at the top of Krahn Hill, just above the tiny island.

The bewildered natives accepted that their tiny island had now been occupied without their prior knowledge or permission.

The natives were also amazed by what appeared to be a column of sheds made with materials they had never seen before—poles covered with hard cloth—and strange-looking people dressed in strange garments.

The natives gathering on the mainland led the newcomers to prepare for war; they fired a few more warning shots. The natives responded with their slingshots to show their ability to defend themselves.

Although the natives' primitive weapons were no match for those of the settlers, their ferocity reminded the settlers of the formidable dangers that they must reckon with in their new environment. As they realized the seriousness of the situation at hand, the natives retreated to their hideouts to avoid further confrontations with their new neighbors. The battle for land occupation had begun in earnest: the natives had lost one of their inviolable places of worship.

The only hope left to their traditional ruler was to protect their mainland from further incursions and to see what the future held for them all.

The Gola tribe, one of the oldest ethnic groups in Liberia, once lived near the coastal regions of the Grain Coast. The fear of the Atlantic slave trade caused the members of the tribe to confine themselves to the deepest forested areas of the country.

Since then, the Gola ethnic group has remained in their dark forests. This is why many people still refer to some areas of Liberia as "Gola forests," particularly in and around the counties of Bomi and Grand Capemount in present-day Liberia.

The name "Gola" is believed to have derived from the word "gorilla." The name was coined by the early Portuguese explorers, who visited the West African coast in the 1460s, where they saw a group of bearded, hairy men. Observing the appearance of these natives, the European explorers described them as 'gorillas.' This name was offensive to many members of the tribe for obvious reasons.

As civilization improved over the years, the three middle letters of the English spelling of Gorilla,' namely r-i-l were omitted, to form the word 'Gola.' This became the new universal name of the tribe.

The Gola ethnic group was believed to have descended from a male elephant, which was why the ancient Gola tribe never ate elephant meat; and a man who grew old and was approaching death was taken to secluded areas of the forest to await his apparent transformation into an elephant.

Ancient Gola folklore related that when Daya (the Gola appellation for 'God') created the Gola tribe, He ordained that: "Elephant thou art; unto elephant, thou ought to return."

For this reason, there were no graveyards for men in Gola settlements in ancient times. Graves found were mainly those of women, or children who had died in the early stages of life.

It was also a tradition that Gola boys who completed their bush training from Poro initiation sessions had to be escorted to town by a male elephant.

The Gola tribe originally shared similar cultures and traditions with other ethnic groups, such as the Vai in Grand Capemount County; the Belleh, Gissi, Lorma, Gbandi, and Mende in Lofa County; and the Kpelleh in Bomi and Bong counties. These tribes all collectively constituted what was known as the "Poro and Sande clusters of Liberia." These were (and still are) powerful civil societies with bush schools for traditional education of boys and girls prior to adulthood and marriage.

The Gola tribe once ruled Lopolu and peacefully intermingled with other ethnic groups. In later years, however, frequent outbreaks of bitter and often bloody inter ethnic conflicts disrupted such peaceful coexistence.

Lopolu, a well-known traditional settlement in the northwestern part of the country, was a town of many characteristics. Its fame rested on the nature of several multidimensional activities that extended beyond the region. Because of the intermittent inter ethnic rivalry between various warring tribes, the town had changed hands among many different ethnic groups.

This rivalry apparently began with the arrival of the Sumba warriors, a notorious band of fighters who invaded the area from the shores of a neighboring country called Sierra Leone. The Sumbas had an insatiable thirst for power and conquest, and left no stone unturned.

They were eventually conquered in a series of wars with the Belleh, Gbandi, Gissi, Gola, Kpelleh, Lorma, and Mende ethnic groups, who each, in turn, created a hegemony, with a display of superiority over the others. Later there was a conflict between the Gola and the Dei ethnic groups, in which the Dei tribe emerged victorious.

Later still, the Kpelleh and Mandingo tribes, who both originated from the coastal regions of French Guinea, where they had escaped the territorial conflicts between the Western European imperialists and the famous native warrior called Samouri, had fought each other to a stalemate. They made peace with each other and made Lopolu their permanent place of abode.

Consequently, Lopolu, along with its outlying towns and villages, became a multilingual society, where nearly everyone spoke most tribal languages.

But there was more to Lopolu than a multichannel region where everyone got along: it was the center for juju activities. People came from far and wide to seek juju protection against their enemies. While some went there for healing purposes, others went there mainly to punish their rivals. Even the more affluent people went there to acquire supernatural powers in order to enhance their daily lives.

Lopolu was a village where any devilish undertaking was possible and at little cost. These characteristics made it a popular place to go in times of necessity. The simple mention of the word "Lopolu" put fear in the minds of ordinary people who had little knowledge about the art of juju.

The more unscrupulous people working in Monrovia often bullied their colleagues at work by boldly telling them, "If you mess with me, you will be a dead man when I get back from Lopolu next weekend."

Despite its juju characteristics, Lopolu was an important trading center. Farmers from the outlying towns and villages brought their agricultural produce there, for bartering on a weekly basis—mainly on Fridays. Goods were exchanged for goods, based on individual needs; little cash was exchanged. A hunter exchanged his meat for rice, while a portion of salt was exchanged for oil. This bartering system of trade continued long after the much later introduction of a modern commercial system of trade involving the use of cash. Because these activities took place on Fridays, many people refrained from farm work, either for religious or other purposes.

ONE

The traditional West African belief system is largely rooted in the influence of the dead over the affairs of the living. If the living respect, remember, and appease their ancestors, their requests to the Supreme God to fulfill their daily earthly needs, through their ancestors, are assured of being accepted.

These earthly needs include a large family, good harvests, long life, good health, and prosperity. The opposite—displeasing one's ancestors—is believed to cause barrenness, accidental deaths, and other forms of misfortune to the living descendants.

One of the spiritual representations of the dead here on Earth is to be found in palm trees; this is why red palm oil, produced from the dates of palm trees, is of paramount necessity in most West African communities in all ceremonies venerating ancestors. Palm trees have similar symbolic spiritual attributes to those of kola trees in most of West Africa. Kola nut, in particular, is so synonymous with traditional marriage ceremonies that even the "bride-price" paid by the groom's family, is still referred to as "white kola." Without this symbolic ritual, the marriage could not be recognized from the traditional point of view.

It is wrongly perceived that black Africans worship their ancestors; this is not necessarily the case. Instead, they remember, honor, and appease their ancestors through some sort of ceremony.

The underlying factor is that humans become spirits upon their death and therefore become closer to the Almighty God, who, according to many universal belief systems, is a supreme spirit who alone exists of Himself and is infinite in all perfection.

Because the dead dwell in the spiritual abode, they are believed to be closer to this Supreme God and therefore are capable of communicating with Him on behalf of their living descendants.

Many West Africans thus appeal to this Supreme God (then and now) through their ancestors to provide for, and guarantee, their social and economic needs here on Earth.

This practice is similar to other universal belief systems, whose members often invoke the spirits of numerous generations of people to intercede to the Almighty God on their behalf during their prayers. Nearly all prayers related to ancestor veneration in West Africa often end with the words, "May God accept our prayers," which implies that such prayers are meant for the Supreme God alone and not necessarily the ancestors per se.

Because the roots of the palm tree descend deeply into the ground—the spiritual abode of the ancestors—palm trees are therefore believed to serve as one of the major symbolic communication links between the living and the dead. Their height extends far above the surface of the Earth into the domain of humans.

Not all prayers offered by the living through their ancestors are believed to be instantly answered by the Supreme God. This is why the living had to appeal so often to their ancestors to remind the Supreme God, through informal ceremonies, to ensure the protection of women and children—particularly boys who are perceived as the major source of maintaining family names through their future sons—from accidental deaths due to snake bites, falling from palm trees, and from fire and drowning.

There is no incontrovertible evidence about how palm trees arrived in West Africa. Historical references suggest, however, that the human use of palm oil may date as far back as five thousand years and that palm oil became a highly sought-after commodity during Britain's Industrial Revolution, starting in the 1780s.

Palm trees grow wild in West Africa, and their dates and physical features are quite different from other palm trees and dates found in North Africa, the Arabian Peninsula, and elsewhere.

Wild palm trees in West Africa are not planted, but their ripe dates are mostly extracted and eaten by birds during harvest seasons; and wherever the seeds are dropped by birds, they grow there.

The lifespan of a palm tree lasts longer than humans'; they may survive up to a century or more if left untouched.

Palm trees produce palm dates, from which edible oil is obtained; their kernels constituted a major source of export for industrial use prior to the discovery of crude oil elsewhere around the globe.

Dates from West African wild palm trees are harvested every six months, using primitive methods including the use of climbers, machetes, and sharp blades. The production of edible palm oil from palm dates is labor intensive (similar to that of primitive methods of subsistence rice farming) in most of West Africa.

The harvesting and processing of ripe palm dates into cooking oil is a household division of labor, in which men risk their lives to climb and cut the dates, and women and children gather the harvested dates beneath the trees, to be taken to processing venues in heavy baskets on their heads, at times far away from the harvesting sites.

At such processing venues, the ripe dates are extracted from their thorny attachments, and women manually process the soft yellow outer coatings to produce red oil for household use. During this process, the extracted kernels are left to dry in the sun and later cracked. The seeds are then roasted in heated containers and mashed in wooden mortals and subsequently processed by the women into edible oil for household use.

Palm trees also have other uses: palm cabbage produced from palm trees constitutes a major source of food in times of hunger for people who cannot afford the high costs of food, especially during the rainy season. Palm trees can also be tapped to produce palm wine, which is widely consumed by both men and women in West Africa.

The leaves and branches of palm trees have symbolic cultural interpretations in Liberia: a display of palm branches on both sides of a vehicle implies that the vehicle is carrying a corpse; and palm fronds displayed in any part of the bush implies that the area is in use for ritual initiation of boys into the male Poro secret society, which is a powerful civil society that trains and transforms boys into adulthood prior to marriage.

Historical references also suggest that during British colonial rule in neighboring Sierra Leone(formerly called "Sierra Lyao"(meaning"Lion Mountains")by the Portuguese explorers, members of the male Poro secret society wore palm fronds around their necks to carry coded messages from village to village, which largely influenced the assembly of able men to fight against the British colonial administration. This was in response to the latter's introduction of the infamous "hut tax," which required every man to pay a tax based on the number of huts occupied by his family members. As polygyny was widespread and was characterized by large family-size, men with many wives and children found it impossible to afford the cost of such taxation. The natives preferred the old "head tax" system, which was more affordable. This issue eventually led to a bloody conflict in 1898 known as the "Hut Tax War."

Branches of palm trees also provide viable building materials for the native populations in West Africa, who use them to roof their farm sheds and barns, which may also be used as dwelling units. Oil produced out of ripe palm dates generates a major source of income for many people to feed and clothe their family members and to cover other household costs.

TWO

Liberia became independent on July 26, 1847 and its rulers soon became entrenched with multiple tasks of nation building. Up to January 1856, the newly independent country was still structuring the modus operandi of its economic apparatus to meet the growing needs of its people:- mainly the new American settlers.

The secretary of state for settlement and land distribution of the Republic of Liberia, the Honorable J. Decimal Johnson, had arrived earlier than usual that morning in his newly furnished office in Monrovia, in expectation of receiving very important guests. As he sat behind his desk, he took out his reading glasses and put them on. He then looked closely at the sketch of a map earlier placed on his desk by his loyal secretary.

Mr. Johnson opened his briefcase and took out a ruler, along with a pencil. He drew a circle around the precise spot on the map that he identified as being the ideal venue for future industrial development purposes. As he did so, there was a gentle knock on the office door by his private secretary, informing him of the arrival of a group of five American businessmen of Negro descent. The secretary of state asked his secretary to let the men in.

As they made their way into the office, they were greeted at the door by their host with friendly handshakes and jovial comments, after which coffee and drinks were served.

"What can I do for you gentlemen?" the secretary of state asked.

The leader of the group, Mr. Anderson, spoke on behalf of his delegation. He told the secretary of state of their intention to invest in the oil palm industry and of the social and economic benefits this would bring to the newly independent nation. Mr. Anderson emphasized that in order to achieve their aspirations, they needed the government's support to acquire a plot of land for such a venture.

These remarks attracted the attention of the secretary of state, who thought for a while before replying. He began by discussing how the issue of land in Liberia was sensitive and contentious, and ended with the associated risks and accrued financial implications involved. He did tell the investors how in the past few weeks he had personally made an effort to identify an area in a settlement called Freeman Town as the ideal venue for the type of industry the investors had in mind. Mr. Johnson concluded that, in view of his personal involvement in the issue, he was willing to make a deal on the acquisition of land, but with the condition that he would become a shareholder within such an investment.

In view of the legal implications involved, Mr. Anderson requested that the meeting be adjourned for a short time in order to seek legal advice and that he and his colleagues would return to conclude their discussions on the issue. This put the investors in a position to either accept or reject what the secretary of state proposed.

As the investors left his office that morning, the secretary of state wondered if he had drawn too sharp of a bargain: one that would drive the investors away. As he pondered the issue, however, there was a gentle knock on his office door by his loyal private secretary, informing him of the arrival of American delegation for the resumption of their adjourned meeting.

As the meeting resumed that afternoon, Mr. Anderson declared that he and his delegation had accepted the condition the secretary of state had proposed during their morning session. This remark brought a big smile to the secretary of state's face.

A moment later, Mr. Anderson presented a white envelope to the secretary of state, containing an undisclosed amount as a gift on behalf of his delegation: a symbolic gesture commonly referred to in Liberia as cold water. The conclusion of this official meeting paved the way for the establishment of the Oil Palm Plantations Company, the first and largest plantation in Liberia.

THREE

The American settlers of Negro descent, often referred to as " Americo-Liberians" or "Congo people," continued to arrive in Liberia in the 1850s, well after the declaration of independence in 1847. Many came from various family backgrounds with diverse names, mostly inherited from their former slave masters in North America and elsewhere. As they found their new homes in Liberia, they began to vie with each other to occupy land. A piece of land, once occupied, was named after the occupier's family: thus, settlements such as Bardnersville, Bensonville, Charlesville, Johnsonville, Gardnersville, and Barclaysville (and hundreds of others like them) were all named under such a system of land acquisition and ownership. Freeman Town became one such settlement.

Freeman Town was founded (no one is quite sure when) by one James Freeman, a member of the early American freed black slave settlers. The new settlement rapidly grew into a sizable community, where nearly everyone carried the Freeman name. Whether related by blood or not, every Freeman claimed to belong to the same ancestry and were therefore accorded preferential treatment over those with names other than Freeman. To maintain the status quo, all appointed magistrates and justices of the peace had to be of Freeman ancestry.

This complex nomenclature made it difficult for ordinary inhabitants in the outlying towns and villages to differentiate between sons and daughters from fathers and mothers within the official hierarchy of Freeman Town.

Freeman Town was also where the initial residential facilities of the Oil Palm Plantations Company were built. As the company became operative over the years (which brought administrative staff and large numbers of manual laborers and their extended family members from across the country), these facilities were relocated to the main administrative headquarters in Division 95.

Through these mechanisms, Freeman Town became a multicultural settlement where ordinary people intermingled with those of Freeman ancestry. This combination of culture and tradition made Freeman Town a popular social venue within the periphery of the Oil Palm Plantations Company.

Freeman Town was also a favorable destination for travelers and other inhabitants from other parts of the country, who came there during weekly market days to buy, sell, or exchange their local produce on the basis of value and quality.

In spite of its economic and social viability, Freeman Town had a dark history. The settlement's judicial system was fundamentally flawed. Its extra-judicial correctional facilities, known by the people as the "No Return Detention Center" (or NRDC, for short), equally made it a fearful place to live. Under this judicial system, there was no logical difference between people who were accused of minor offenses and those who committed serious crimes: both were arbitrarily sent to prison without due process of law.

Those confined for specified prison terms remained there at the pleasure of the local authorities long after their prison terms had ended.

There was also something much more sinister about the NRDC. It operated a ritual practice in which prisoners slated for release were only released at midnight: and those released were uncertain to make it to their original homes again. Instead, such unfortunates mysteriously disappeared under the cover of darkness.

The practice of having many wives and concubines was widespread among those of Freeman ancestry. The most common offenses for which people were imprisoned ranged from having illicit sexual relationships with the wives or concubines of the Freeman family to making pejorative remarks against local authorities.

As a result, people with many wives and concubines began to encourage their partners to seduce vulnerable manual laborers and later to confess the act: a culture commonly referred to as "kiss and tell." Such offenses carried heavy fines, locally referred to as "woman damage." Those who could afford to pay this "woman damage" were spared from going to prison. Those who could not often found themselves confined to the NRDC indefinitely. These extra-judicial practices continued unabated for decades.

One sunny Saturday afternoon in 1878, however, a notorious robber arrived in Freeman Town during one of its busiest open market days. The man's name was known simply as "Ringo," as no one knew his real name.

He was a giant of a man who at times used his flexible hands to snatch money from under the tablecloth of market women without being noticed. When stealth was not possible, Ringo used violence to achieve his aims. Ringo had harassed market women in Monrovia's waterfront market for decades with impunity, thus prompting his victims there to give him the popular nickname "Don't Blame God." This was because women who were robbed often cried out, "Oh my God!" Ringo simply replied, "Don't blame God! Blame me!"

Ringo had received a tip-off from his underground informants in Monrovia that the Oil Palm Plantations workers often got paid on open market days, which fell on Saturdays. And that such pay day seasons brought a substantial flow of cash from plantation workers to the head of the newly founded Church organization. He decided to come there to discover what the market day had to offer and to also exploit an avenue of how to infiltrate the functions of the new Church organization for possible financial gains.

The women at the Freeman Town market did not know for certain who Ringo was, until around midday that Saturday. Ringo approached the first table in the market he came to and asked the woman, "Your money or your life?"

Thinking that he was armed, the woman quickly surrendered her cash. Ringo then approached the second table and repeated the same to the next woman. This time his serendipity ran out. Armed officers of the Plantations Protection Force had been called in by market goers who only moments earlier had witnessed the first crime being committed; Ringo was arrested and sent to NRDC without trial.

While in prison, Ringo would do more good than harm, which was to have a lasting impact on the entire judicial system in Freeman Town. Immediately following his arrest, Ringo organized a clandestine criminal network, operated through his agents in Monrovia, who began to smuggle in locally distilled gin (popularly known as "cane juice") for their incarcerated comrade at the NRDC.

Ringo then used these smuggled drinks to entertain not only his fellow inmates, but also the two prison guards assigned to NRDC. Ringo's generosity soon caused the prison guards to become so dependent on his gifts that they expected to have free drinks on a daily basis. In so doing, the prison guards neglected to keep their eyes on Ringo, who instead was allowed to roam about the prison yard at will.

Ringo discovered through some sources that the builders and engineers who constructed NRDC were held as hostages during and after the construction of the notorious prison: a deterrent used to conceal the nature of the prison to common outsiders. These individuals later managed to escape through a clandestine route they dug within the prison compound. With this in mind, Ringo was therefore, eager to know how these builders and engineers managed to escape. Within a short period of time, Ringo had discovered this escape route in the cellars of the prison yard.

Ringo also observed that the entrance gates to the prison yard, manned by armed prison guards, led to the base of the notorious Freeman Town Local Defense Force. This made it impossible for any prisoner to escape through the entrance gates without been caught or possibly shot dead.

Ringo therefore, experimented with the escape route alone several times to ensure that it was safe enough for his fellow inmates to escape without danger.

Ringo kept this discovery a guarded secret, away from his inmates. One evening, his agents in Monrovia smuggled a large quantity of strong alcohol into Ringo's prison cell. Ringo sought to supply the prison guards first, before his fellow inmates. Ringo continued this type of generosity to the prison guards on a regular basis in subsequent weeks, hoping this would instill confidence in him.

One afternoon, Ringo's generosity got the best of him, and he offered the prison guards more drinks than was strictly necessary. They became intoxicated and neglected their official duties in the prison yard. Sensing their intoxication, Ringo politely requested that the two drunken men allow his fellow inmates to celebrate his birthday that very evening. The two prison guards granted their permission with slurred speech.

After sharing a few jokes with the prison guards at his expense about his upcoming birthday celebration, Ringo stayed with them until they both fell asleep. As they lay sleeping, Ringo made a brief announcement to his fellow inmates. He told them that he was now effectively in charge of the prison yard and that everyone was free to go without fear. He personally led all sixty-five prisoners at NRDC to their escape route and set them free. But Ringo himself didn't leave, and the escapees never bothered to ask him why.

Ringo assured himself that, since the local authorities in Freeman Town had detained him without trial for an indefinite period, therefore, he could not, under any circumstances, leave the prison yard until otherwise ordered by those who had sent him there. As the other prisoners escaped, Ringo returned to his prison cell and locked himself up to sleep for the night.

The next morning, when the prison guards emerged from their intoxication, they found to their horror that every prisoner in the No Return Detention Center would, in fact, return to their homes. They found Ringo fast asleep in his cell. The two guards stood over Ringo and began to blame each other for the prisoners' escape. Their exchange of words soon woke him up. Ringo asked, "What's the matter, my good friends?"

The bewildered prison guards told Ringo that all of his fellow inmates had escaped during the night. Ringo asked, "And where were you both?"

As the guards could not give a definitive answer to his question, Ringo simply remarked, "I wish I had known to escape with them."

As the prisoners made their escape, they avoided every suspicion that would endanger their safety. They therefore, used various routes in the bush to make their ways into the countryside. There, they became a major source of information to the local populations about the establishments of the oil palm plantations company and the notorious correction center known as"No Return Detention Center" in Freeman Town. The dimension which paved the way for the company's future recruitment of manual laborers from the countryside.

The news of the prisoners escape from the NRDC quickly spread like wildfire, far beyond the Oil Palm Plantations Company.

As the national newspaper, *The Oracle*, broke the news in its editorial the next morning, the local authorities ordered an immediate closure of the notorious prison camp, and Ringo became the first prisoner ever to be officially set free in broad daylight from the NRDC. From that day on, Freeman Town became a normal functioning society.

As the episode unfolded, the local authorities in Freeman Town approached the newly released prisoner with the hope of using his expertise to their advantage. With the escape of all prisoners, the authorities feared the emergence of other forms of criminal activities in Freeman Town. To them, only criminals can effectively locate where other criminals resided, and Ringo being a criminal himself, was no exception. The authorities therefore, decided to use Ringo's expertise to curb criminal activities in their community. This initially however, was difficult as the official hierarchy in Freeman Town had always been associated with the Freeman ancestry to which Ringo did not belong. Furthermore, Ringo was a man of criminal history and by bringing him closer to the hierarchy would be counter-productive.

After intense deliberations, it was unanimously decided that Ringo should become the new police commander incognito, thereby concealing his natural identity. This required Ringo to wear full official police uniforms at all times within the confines of Freeman Town. Thus, Ringo became the new commander of Freeman Town Police Detachment while his predecessor was promoted to a new post of land commissioner of Freeman Town.

Ringo's appointment brought huge social and economic benefits to Freeman Town but not without a price. Ringo became so efficient in his new job that he would locate and retrieve any stolen items other than cash, based on quality as long as the victims were ready to pay the fee requested to retrieve their stolen items. Stolen cash of any value was not part of this bargain, the money retrieved went to the coffers of the new police commander. For instance, a sewing machine stolen from a resident in Freeman Town would be located and retrieved from Monrovia at a cost of fifteen US dollars; while a stolen country garment mostly worn by prominent tribal leaders, would be located and retrieved from another local village at a cost of ten US dollars. How these stolen items were located and retrieved by the flamboyant police commander remained a mystery.

In spite of Ringo's concealed identity, many local residents soon realized that the new police commander was a man of criminal characteristics.

FOUR

The area in Freeman Town set aside for the Oil Palm Plantations Company in 1856 had been cleared when the first shipment of nursery palm trees arrived to be planted. The planted nursery palm trees could take up to seventeen years before they could mature to produce the first dates.

Nearly eighteen years had passed since the first nursery palm trees had been planted, and they began to produce dates to be harvested. The company gradually expanded into 100 divisions of which Division 95 became its headquarters. The company had begun in earnest.

There was an acute shortage of manual labor to harvest and process the ripe palm dates into palm oil, however, and this category of workforce could not be recruited among the new settler community, who were not by any means accustomed to manual work in the heat of the sun.

It thus became imperative for the management to devise a strategy that would attract indigenous rural populations of the country for such servitude. To ensure this goal, the company introduced the allocation of free housing and a monthly supply of a bag of American parboiled rice, locally referred to as pussawa,for its employees. The strategy worked, and soon there was a mass exodus of natives from the rural areas of Liberia to the newly established oil palm plantations.

As the company came into full operation, the management built and operated a free health care unit, with its facilities located in Division 95, the administrative headquarters of the company. Although the health care clinic soon became especially famous, this fame did not rest entirely on the quality of medical care received by its patients. Rather, it was based on the notoriety of its only medical doctor, called "Doctor Turn Around" by the people. He was called this because each patient who visited his clinic was simply told to "turn around" for an injection in the buttocks, without a medical checkup to ascertain the actual nature of the illness. Patients who were given injections often experienced severe pains lasting several days before they could recover. Whether this was due to the effectiveness of Dr. Turn Around's medication or otherwise remained a mystery.

As the plantation brought a large segment of rural inhabitants, many people who by now had abandoned their traditional belief practices from their original settlements to work for the plantation converted (at least on the surface) to Christianity. Consequently, they were eager to attend church services on a regular basis, outside of their working hours.

Based on popular demands by this category of workers, the management sought to create a "spiritual branch" within the Oil Palm Plantations Company.

This strategy attracted the founder of the newly established African Church of the Apostolic Faith, the Right Reverend Jeremiah.

Reverend Jeremiah had been an influential figure in the settlement of Freeman Town prior to the company's operation. His regular open-air preaching activities, especially during Freeman Town's open market days (which coincided with the company's payday period), brought large numbers of people together in the community. This venture earned the reverend a substantial income.

Through this venture, the management officially endorsed Reverend Jeremiah as the spiritual voice of the company, with lucrative incentives. These included a well furnished bungalow, a company car, and a spacious warehouse, which became the headquarters of his newly founded Christian organization.

These incentives caused the reverend to scale down his spiritual base in the settlement of Freeman Town and to permanently move to the company's headquarters in Division 95. This spiritual role effectively placed the reverend in parity with most senior management officials in the plantations. He subsequently began to exercise a form of nepotistic influence over the plantation managers by recommending friends and relatives for employment opportunities or promotions, regardless of their qualifications or experiences. The system soon became part of his *modus operandi.*

FIVE

Among West Africa's traditional indigenous populations, stable marriage provided the basis for people to have a normal family life. This was mainly to produce and rear children who would later in life look after, and provide for, their parents and grandparents within the wider extended family structure.

This was necessary because, in the absence of modern-day social security benefits, children were seen as the major source of such security in old age for most families. Stable marriage was therefore a social necessity to ensure such filial piety.

For Joe Blackee, however, this was not the state of affairs that he knew. Born to a chieftaincy family in northeastern Liberia, Joe had undergone proper traditional training in subsistence rice farming and the art of hunting and climbing palm trees. These skills were necessary for every male child born in the community.

Joe's birth name was Fatoma Nyandemoh. The second part of his name is the Gbandi and Mende appellation for "Handsome Man." Fatoma was born in a village founded by his grandfather, the famous Chief Nyandemoh. Soon after its founding, people began to call the village "Nyandemoh-Lahun," meaning "Handsome Man's Town."

In his early childhood, Fatoma loved wearing black shorts and black shirts, and people began to call him Joe Blackee, a name he cherished and adopted for the rest of his life.

Joe's problems started on the evening when he caught his newly wedded wife in bed with another man. Aggrieved by this event, Joe successfully sought the nullification of the marriage through a traditional process and had finally put the issue behind him. He subsequently married another woman, who produced two sons. As a result of his frequent (and often prolonged) absences from his village, however, Joe one day returned home and found his second wife heavily pregnant.

As she had shown no sign of pregnancy prior to his departure from the village several months earlier, Joe was convinced that such a pregnancy could not have been by him. He thus requested the elders to again nullify the marriage. They turned down his request on traditional grounds, as the dissolution of a marriage while a woman remained pregnant was forbidden.

While waiting for the pregnancy to take its course, Joe became a laughing stock to most of his comrades, many of whom considered him to be impotent.

Some maintained that Joe compensated his social ailment by blindly encouraging other men to have illicit affairs with his wives, as he was clearly incapable of copulating. Others pointed out that the two sons of his wife were not biologically his, but since a married woman could not by definition produce illegitimate children within the traditional African family structure, Joe was obliged to accept the children as his.

Amid these innuendos, Joe's estranged wife one morning gave birth to a bouncing baby girl. There was no physical resemblance between Joe and the newborn child. The village midwife was also quick to reveal that, during delivery, the mother-to-be had confessed to her that Joe was not actually the biological father of the newborn child. This revelation largely influenced the elders to nullify the marriage, which paved the way for Joe to finally leave his beloved village. He would begin a new life elsewhere in Liberia.

Anger and frustration at times create impenetrable barriers especially when a man faces social disappointments in life. Joe was forced to abandoned his two sons in his home village but deep down in his heart, he was convinced that they would one day be reunited in life: but this became more remote when Joe left his beloved village and permanently settled in the plantations.

SIX

Like the biblical children of Israel in Egypt, following their redemption by God through the Prophet Moses, Joe at first knew not where to go.

As he thought about his predicament, however, he soon recollected the Oil Palm Plantations Company in Freeman Town he had heard so much about. He had heard stories from a number of itinerant travelers who had stopped by his village in the past about a large oil palm plantation where manual work was easily attainable by aspiring job-seekers.

He had gathered from the travelers including the escaped prisoners from the notorious prison camp in Freeman Town, that the new plantations provided free housing and a free monthly supply of rice as incentives to manual laborers. He was enthusiastic to seek employment there, as he had been brought up in a society where rice was a staple food. Joe loved rice and had always produced it in abundance to feed his entire family, in the village and beyond.

When he was a child, Joe had often heard his grandfather say, you can play with my money, you can play with my wives, and you can play with my children. But do not play with my rice. For the day I die, the only thing I take to my grave will be the grain of rice in my stomach.

Because of his love for rice, Joe's comrades in the village often provoked him by saying that "where there was rice, there was Joe; and where there was Joe, there was rice." Joe equally loved his village, like any other man born and bred in rural Liberia.

Ancient traditional folklore related that:

One man is not a nation;
One tree cannot make a forest; and
One stone cannot be called a mountain.

You can take the fish away from the river,
But you can never take the river away from the fish.

You can take the animal away from the bush;
But you can never take the bush away from the animal.

And you can take the boy away from the village;
But you can never take the village away from the boy.

Joe had always remained patriotic to his village, and the community never had a cause to banish him. For Joe to permanently leave his beloved village for reasons other than banishment was a sad state of affairs. As Euripides once said, "There is no greater sorrow on Earth than to lose one's place of birth."

Joe had left his village with no valuables except for a bundle of personal effects; there was no road connecting his village with the rest of the country. Joe had to walk to his intended destination.

The journey was dangerous. He had heard terrifying stories from a number of travelers, who told him of vicious men who roamed the dense forests at night to abduct and kill lone travelers for ritualistic purposes.

There were also fearsome wild animals such as lions, buffaloes, and leopards, which roamed the countryside and threatened travelers at night. Determination is the key to success, however, and determination knows no fear. Joe was determined to make the journey at all costs: even his own life. He was fond of saying, "No one died before his appointed time!"

SEVEN

Dusk had spread its protruding darkness over Liberia and the Atlantic Ocean beyond when Joe arrived at the Oil Palm Plantations Company. His first sighting was a little hamlet occupied by the headman of what Joe perceived to be a handful of casual laborers within the company.

Because there had been two attempted burglaries in the headman's hamlet in the past few payday seasons, however, he could not allow another. He was certain that none of the denizens of his hamlet had told him of the arrival of a relative or friend that night. He was suspicious of the newcomer.

Relaxing in his old raffia hammock outside the veranda of the little hut, smoking his wooden pipe, the headman spotted a lit cane torch coming toward him. In total readiness for the inevitable confrontation, he grabbed his machete and shouted in his best authoritative voice: "Stop where you are! Who are you?"

Joe lowered his torch to the ground and said, "My name is Joe Blackee. I've come to look for work in the oil palm plantations."

Do you know anyone here? shouted the headman. Joe replied in the negative, informing the headman that he had never been to the plantations.

As a gesture of friendship and hospitality to a stranger, the headman invited Joe to the veranda of his windowless mud hut. Following a few friendly exchanges, he offered Joe hot water to take a bath, followed by food and a spare room in which to spend the night.

Before retiring for the night, Joe asked politely of his host, "I'd like to find a job in this plantation; do you know anyone who could help?"

The headman scratched his head several times and thought for a while before giving a definitive answer. He stated that if Joe were serious about seeking employment in the plantations, then he, as the headman in the area, would be willing to accompany him to the employment center first thing in the morning. Joe unreservedly accepted this kind offer.

It was barely five o'clock the following morning when the headman and Joe arrived at a small, overcrowded office at the Oil Palm Plantations Company. There, they met a crowd of aspiring job seekers.

As a well-known figure within the hierarchy of the oil palm plantations, the headman was given the first opportunity to see the recruitment manager, commonly known as Bobby.

As Joe and the headman emerged from the office, Bobby requested that Joe should spend the rest of the day with the headman in a shadowing capacity in order to familiarize himself with the daily activities required of every manual laborer in the plantations.

By the end of his first working day, a messenger arrived with a simple handwritten note from Bobby to the headman, instructing him to take Joe to the housing officer in Division 80 Housing Unit the following morning to provide a home for the new employee. The following day, Joe became a fully fledged manual laborer in the Division 80 Housing Unit within the Oil Palm Plantations Company. There, he was to live and work continuously for the next twenty-two years.

EIGHT

Joe had lived and worked in Division 80 Housing Unit for seventeen years. Most of his next door neighbors in the housing unit were not only born in the plantations, but had lived and served the company for more than three decades. As a man who had experienced hardship and pleasure as two sides of the same coin, Joe was a regular customer at Camp Nennie, a popular drinking establishment where most of the manual laborers working for the country's largest plantations gathered in the evenings after their work was done to consume bamboo wine.

His daily visit to Camp Nennie, coupled with the fact that he never passed anyone without a smile, meant that Joe soon became one of the most celebrated employees in the plantations and beyond. Joe had the ability to speak nearly every tribal language of his country. As a result, it was difficult to pin him to any one particular ethnic group.

No one knew how, where, or when he obtained the knowledge of so many languages. One thing was for certain, however: wherever Joe went or settled in Liberia, the people of that settlement considered him to be one of their own. Joe entered the Oil Palm Plantations well-endowed with natural instincts, which quickly enhanced his social popularity among his comrades. Despite these fine attributes, many people were puzzled about why Joe didn't have a wife in the plantations. Some of his friends secretly gossiped that Joe was impotent: the same type of gossip he had endured in his own village prior to his arrival in the plantations. He jovially brushed aside such notions and simply said, "God's time is the best."

Many others considered Joe to be an ordinary drinking pal, who simply wanted to enjoy himself without offending anyone.

Joe was returning home late one evening from one of his routine wine-drinking evenings when he came across a woman wandering in the dark not far from his home. He stumbled over her. From the moment Joe spotted her, he rightly predicted that, "To bring in a woman to his life for the third time was to bring in more trouble."

He took the risk and greeted the woman in the Kpelleh tribal language; she replied in the Gola vernacular. Being multilingual, Joe quickly inquired of the woman in perfect Gola about what she was doing out in the dark like this. The woman replied that she had come all the way from Lopolu to look for an uncle who had for many years worked for the Oil Palm Plantations Company.

As the stranger was providing a description of her uncle, Joe held her right hand to say that the man she was looking for had been a good friend of his, but that unfortunately he had died two years ago: precisely six months after his retirement. The woman began to weep. "Oh! My God, where can I go now, since I know no one in this plantation? Where can I find someone to stay with? And what can I do now?"

Joe began to console the woman as best as he could. He invited her to his dwelling to spend the night, and she agreed.

As they arrived home, Joe made a fire in the outside kitchen in order to make hot water for the stranger to take a bath and to cook a meal for her.

Once the water was hot, Joe poured it into a large galvanized bucket and took it to a nearby outdoor makeshift bathroom built with palm branches. While the stranger was taking her bath, Joe opened his cupboard and took out a large cooking container. He carefully washed the container and poured a good quantity of water into it. He then placed the container on the fire to cook some rice for his guest.

As the stranger emerged from the bathroom, she took over the cooking activities. To her, cooking was a woman's task, which was a great relief to Joe. Joe became silent for a while. The woman, too, was initially very shy to start a full conversation, as they had never met. As the cooking progressed, the woman took the initiative to break the silence by politely asking whether Joe was a married man; he instantly replied in the negative.

"You haven't yet told me your name," Joe remarked.

"Well, why didn't you ask when we first met this evening? the stranger jovially remarked. Anyway, my name is Jenneh. Jenneh Dao."

"Is Dao your father's name, or the name of your husband?" Joe inquired further, with curiosity. "it is my father's name," replied the stranger.

"Are you a married woman?" Joe asked again. "My husband died five years ago. Since then, I haven't found any man to marry me. That is why my father requested for me to come and look for my uncle here at the plantations. He thought his brother would help to find someone to marry me. But now you've just informed me that he has passed away." The stranger wept again, more quietly this time.

Even after such brief social interaction, Joe was now convinced that the long-awaited answer to his prayers to find a faithful and stable wife in life had finally materialized. As Jenneh continued her cooking in the kitchen, Joe went to his bedroom and was initially going to put on a long native robe to impress his guest. Instead, he soon emerged with an old raffia bag hanging over his shoulder and politely asked Jenneh if he could buy her a drink.

"Buy me a drink? Oh! Yes. It is not really my regular habit, but I sometimes prefer Pioneer's Gin," Jenneh remarked.

Joe took a quick walk to a nearby local shop, where he purchased four bottles of Pioneer's Gin and a bottle of Coke. He then made his way back home as fast as he could. By the time he got home, Jenneh had already dished out the rice and had taken the food to the dining table for them to eat out of the same bowl with their bare hands, as tradition dictated.

While they were eating, Joe remarked that Jenneh was the best cook he had ever met. The statement made the stranger smile for the first time since she'd received the news of her uncle's death.

At the dining table, Joe and Jenneh continued to exchange further views on various social issues ranging from ordinary life experiences to family lineage and culture. With their conversations now running along personal levels, Joe took out the first bottle of the gin along with the Coke and passed it over to his guest.

As Jenneh accepted the drink, Joe realized that there was no container from which she could drink. He rushed to his bedroom and brought out a large drinking mug. As Joe returned with the mug, he observed that Jenneh had already drunk the entire contents of the first bottle of gin, without waiting for the Coke.

He then opened the second bottle to pour it into the mug for his guest to drink, as he had already had enough of his daily bamboo wine that evening. Before he could pour the drink, however, Jenneh got hold of Joe's wrist to say that she had always preferred drinking directly from the bottle since the day of her puberty rites and would continue to do so until the end of her days.

At this stage, Joe passed her the second bottle of gin he had already opened. To minimize her embarrassment, Jenneh then began to drink in what appeared to be a normal way. Before long, the second bottle of gin was empty, and Joe was becoming seriously concerned. He feared for her safety if she continued drinking like this. He also feared how the stranger's unpredictable behavior would affect his livelihood in the oil palm plantations, especially if she happened to die in his home as a result of excessive drinking.

With this in mind, Joe was just about to ask Jenneh why she liked drinking without Coke when the stranger unexpectedly remarked, "Don't get me wrong. You and I could drink the whole night, and I will be the first to wake up in the morning, sober enough to do the domestic work: for where I come from, drinking is our hobby. It helps us regain our strength after our daily activities on the farm, and it enhances our conjugal duties at night." Jenneh's remarks encouraged Joe to take out the third bottle of gin. He passed it over to her.

Joe thought his guest had already had enough to drink and decided to take the fourth bottle of gin to his bedroom for safekeeping until the next day. His good intentions had to be abandoned, however, when she asked if there were any more drinks left. Joe retrieved the last bottle of gin from the room in order to appease his guest.

It was getting late, and Joe had to go to work early the next morning. He politely invited Jenneh to go to bed, but this invitation fell on deaf ears. Instead, Jenneh only gave a brief smile and in a level tone of voice, she asked, "Why did you have to take the gin into your bedroom while I was still in a drinking mood?"

Joe apologized to her and stated that he'd wanted to keep the remaining bottle of gin in the room for her to drink the following day while he was away at work.

With that, Jenneh got up and walked to the makeshift bathroom behind the kitchen. As she returned to the dining table, she stood with arms akimbo and firmly said to Joe's face, "I don't drink during the day, and I don't bother when there is nothing to drink. But when I'm in the mood to drink, I make sure the last bottle is empty before I get ready for bed." Joe had no further comments.

Earlier in the evening, while his guest was busy cooking, Joe had put a straw mat beneath his bed where he would be able to sleep so that he could give up his own bed for his guest. This was a traditional generosity to extend to a female stranger.

Since his earlier request for Jenneh to go to bed had fallen on deaf ears, Joe thought that the best idea was for him to be the first to go to bed. He was certain that this would encourage his guest to follow suit, as there was no one else to keep her company. But when Jenneh finally entered the bedroom and found Joe flat on his back on the straw-covered floor, she burst out laughing and said to him,

"Do you really expect me to sleep in that bed alone after giving me all those drinks tonight? Don't let me suggest to you the true reason why you don't have a wife."

Prompt action is often met with prompt reaction. Upon hearing his guest's remarks, Joe got up and dismantled his straw mat. He jumped into bed with his new found-friend. The couple woke up the next morning as if they had been married for decades.

Within ninety days, as provided under the Domestic Relations Law of Liberia at the time, Joe and Jenneh legally became husband and wife.

NINE

Five years had elapsed since Jenneh settled with Joe in the Oil Palm Plantations Company. The couple had lived a peaceful, conjugal life and were regarded as the plantation's most stable social couple.

Through persistent rumors, however, Joe began to suspect an extramarital relationship between his wife and the area manager, under whose supervision he had worked for over two decades. He came to discover that his wife was brought home every evening in a van owned and driven by a Mr. Gabriel Francis. A close friend informed Joe one evening that Mr. Francis knew the actual time Joe was due home and made sure that he dropped Jenneh home every evening before that time.

Though he was aware of the issue through such rumors, Joe was uncertain about his wife's infidelity, as he had not personally seen it happen. He decided to overlook the issue, at least for the time being. God reveals things to his creatures in different and mysterious ways, he told himself.

Joe had several complicated dreams one night. When he awoke the next morning, he experienced many discomforting feelings. He began to sweat profusely and lost his appetite for breakfast. Jenneh, who had attentively observed her husband's movements that morning, could not comprehend what had happened.

She had never seen Joe going to work on an empty stomach since they had met. As Joe took his old raffia bag from the bedroom to go to work early that morning, he tripped twice and fell over his doorstep. He rose to his feet and left for work.

A few yards away from the house, Joe felt the palm of his right hand burning, as if a heated charcoal had been placed there. He could not pinpoint the importance of these events. He thought for a while.

Having been brought up with strong cultural beliefs in his native settlement, Joe assumed that for a man to trip and fall over his doorstep in the early hours of the morning, and subsequently to experience a burning in the palm of his right hand, heralded impending news of a disastrous nature, with far-reaching consequences. He decided not to visit Camp Nennie, at least for the next few days, until he could establish what the dreams and the incidents held in store for him.

Joe returned home from work much earlier than usual that evening: well before his wife, who sold provisions at the nearby plantations market in Division 95. As he entered his bedroom, Joe heard a loud knock on the door of his house. He rightly guessed that something serious was amiss, as none of his next door neighbors had ever knocked on his door since he started employment in the plantations.

As he opened the door, the caller handed him a letter in a large brown envelope with a special message that he must read its contents before going to bed that night.

Curiosity overtook him as he took the letter from the caller. He couldn't imagine what the contents of the letter might say.

Although he considered himself to be a man without an immediate family (other than Jenneh) in the plantations, his first thought went to his two sons he had left behind in his village with his divorced wife some twenty-two years earlier. Could the letter contain news of the death of either of his children? Joe couldn't tell until the whole contents of the letter had been made clear to him. Because he was unable to read or write English, Joe made his way to the home of the primary school teacher, Mr. Aaron Jones, to ask him to read and translate the letter to him in the Kpelleh language, which was widely spoken by many inhabitants in the plantations.

Joe greeted Mr. Jones in a friendly manner in Kpelleh, as he usually did, before explaining the reason for his late evening visit. Mr. Jones took the letter from Joe and opened the envelope. He took out a typewritten letter before taking a brief look at its contents. He then checked the left pocket of his coat to get hold of his reading glasses. Mr. Jones then glanced through the letter, which read:

Dear Mr. Joe Blackee:

Upon the recommendation of your area manager, Mr. Gabriel Francis, we wish to inform you that your service with the Oil Palm Plantations Company as a manual laborer has now reached the stage of retirement.

Under the terms of our agreement, you will upon retirement be entitled to a payment of twenty US dollars every two weeks, but your monthly allocation of a 100-pound bag of rice will be withdrawn immediately. You are also required to surrender your dwelling in Area A of Division 80 within the next six months as of your retirement date, which comes into effect within seven days of the receipt of this letter.

In order to keep you physically and mentally fit following your hard-working years with this company, you will be required to undergo a free medical checkup, followed by a compulsory injection for communicable diseases within the first four days of your retirement. In this context, you are required to immediately report to the Company's health center in Division 95 for the above events with our designated health care specialist, Dr. Turn Around.

The management, as well as the entire clerical staff and laborers of the Oil Palm Plantations Company, wish to thank you for the excellent service you have rendered over the past twenty-two years with the company.

It is with great regret that we must end your valued services with the company. If you have any queries, please do not hesitate to contact your immediate area manager, Mr. Gabriel Francis. Kindest regards.

Yours sincerely,

J. Volgan Barnett

General Manager

As Mr. Jones read and explained the letter to him in Kpelleh, Joe became very uneasy. His legs and hands began to shake violently. He took the letter from Mr. Jones and even forgot to say "thank you," which was not his usual habit. He made his way back to his house.

From the contents of the letter, he could now guess the true meaning of his dreams of the previous night and the two unusual events the following morning. He began to weep, as if his mother had just passed away.

As Joe walked back to his house, he began to ask himself several questions, with tears running down both cheeks: "Why me? What about my other friends who worked for the company over many decades before me? Are they not older than me? Am I not just entering my middle age? Is this the way to reward a hard-working laborer in the plantations after twenty-two unbroken years of service? Did the management check my daily attendance records to see if I had been absent from work, even for a single day? Have any of the managers ever complained about insubordination? Have I ever knowingly insulted any of my colleagues in the plantations?"

As he arrived home, Joe opened the door of his bedroom and entered. He sat down at the lower edge of the bed and held his head with both hands. His grief was greater than he could bear as he awaited the arrival of his wife. How was he going to break this sad news to her?*!!*

Their neighbors in Division 80 generally knew Jenneh as a housewife who sold goods at the main oil palm plantations market in Division 95 to augment the family income. Jenneh came home as usual, a little after sunset, to prepare the evening meal. Normally, upon her return, she put the food basket containing the items she was going to cook that evening down in the outside kitchen.

On this particular evening, however, while walking toward the main door of their house, Jenneh realized that the padlock was not on the door. She stood up and took a long, deep breath. She began to wonder if an intruder had forced open the padlock to steal valuables while she and her husband were away working.

Her apprehension temporarily faded away when she pushed the door open and saw Joe, holding his head with both hands, with tears running down his cheeks. Things must be worse than she feared!

What is the matter, darling? Have we had bad news? Without a word, Joe wiped his face with the palm of his left hand and took out the brown folded envelope containing the letter from his right T-shirt pocket. He sat down next to his wife and began to read the translated version of the letter to her.

After listening to her husband, Jenneh burst into absurd laughter when Joe mentioned that he was to be retired within seven days. She scoffed: "Retired? But you're still a young man! You are telling me that the letter says you will be retired within seven days? Have any of your friends been forced to retire since I came here five years ago? I know from experience that plantation workers are only made to retire when they become too old to carry tins of oil on their heads. Are you sure you have not been fired for bad behavior, or getting drunk on the job?"

Joe stood up and looked her straight in the eye. He said, "How many times has anyone brought a complaint to you about my bad behavior since we met? Have you ever seen me drunk in the morning hours before going to work? Do I ever drink bamboo wine during the day? Mr. Jones read and translated the contents of this letter to me this evening in Kpelleh, and I have just related it to you in Gola since your Kpelleh is still not good. You can go now and ask him if I am lying to you."

Jenneh shook her head in disbelief. She first stood up to go into the kitchen, but then changed her mind. She held the edge of the door with her left hand and her back facing the bedroom. She then turned to her husband and asked a few more provocative questions. She began with the issue of the monthly allocation of a 100-pound bag of rice and ended with the amount of money Joe was entitled to.

As she attempted to leave the room, Joe cajoled his wife, explaining to her in a polite manner that although he had been unexpectedly retired, he would still get an allowance of twenty dollars every two weeks. But his monthly allocation of a 100-pound bag of rice would be withdrawn almost immediately.

Jenneh angrily sucked her teeth at Joe and asked another provocative question: "And where will the rice be coming from to feed you? The twenty dollars will not be enough to buy a bag of rice, provide the ingredients for cooking, and at the same time facilitate your daily wine drinking habit. I think it is time that I went back to my people before I perish on this plantation." Joe was shocked to hear these angry words from his wife. He had expected her to be more sympathetic and to share his sorrow over the news of his unexpected retirement. Her uncompromising remarks caused Joe to lose his temper for the first time, especially when she mentioned going back to her people. He started to talk loudly in a way he had never done before. Joe stood up to his full height to face Jenneh, remarking, "it's only now that you're talking about your people. When I found you wandering in the dark five years ago, you had no one to help you besides me. You could have been abducted by evil-minded men. You cried to me when I broke the sad news of your uncle's death, and I didn't let you down. Tonight, when I've lost my livelihood in the plantations, you want to leave me, to go back to your people. How many relatives of yours have ever visited us since you arrived here five years ago?"

"Oh!" he continued. "In case I forget, you are concerned about losing a bag of rice supplied by the company. There is something much more serious than that. I've got to surrender this house to the company within six months as of today. After that there will be no roof over our head. But you will not be around anyway."

Joe sat down at the edge of his bed. He took his wooden pipe from his old raffia bag. He loaded the pipe with some tobacco, lit it, and began to smoke, before walking away from Jenneh.

TEN

There had been no meaningful interaction between Joe and his wife since he received his letter of enforced retirement. A few days later, however, a male stranger arrived in Division 80 Housing Unit looking for a relative called Jenneh.

The man was led to Joe's house by one of the next door neighbors. Joe had never visited the hometown of his now-estranged wife and found it impossible to distinguish between a blood relative and a lover. He remembered Jenneh telling him on the night of her arrival, however, that she hailed from an ancient town called Lopolu. Reflecting on the basis of this information, Joe politely asked the stranger to properly introduce himself and to explain the purpose of his unannounced visit.

"My name is Momolu Dao, and I've come to look for my younger sister, called Jenneh Dao, who left our village five years ago."

Although Joe knew about his wife's father, Jenneh had never actually talked about her siblings in Lopolu, let alone an elder brother. As a result, Joe found it difficult to accept the stranger's explanation of events. He did, however, tell the stranger that he was now traditionally the lawful husband of Jenneh. Despite their domestic difficulties, Joe decided to wholeheartedly welcome Jenneh's previously unheard-of relative into his dwelling in the plantations.

A few hours later, Jenneh appeared on the road with a basket of food items on her head. At this stage, the stranger stood up with a smile and ran to meet her. They hugged each other in a manner that seemed strange to Joe between siblings; and for whatever reason, Jenneh decided not to introduce her brother to Joe.

That evening, Jenneh cooked an elaborate meal for the stranger, which Joe described as her best since their marriage. The aroma alone from the kitchen instantly caused the next door neighbors to refer to Joe's house as "smell no taste," literally meaning, to "smell but not necessarily eat what was being cooked."

As the evening progressed, Joe decided to prepare a makeshift bed in the kitchen for their own use in order to accommodate the stranger in their normal bedroom. The ensuing romantic exchanges between Jenneh and her pretended brother, however, soon became a source of serious concern for Joe. In the end, he decided to put the stranger's integrity to a small test. Before retiring to their makeshift bed in the kitchen that night, Joe deliberately placed his wooden pipe beneath the bed of their main room where the stranger was to sleep. In the early hours of the following morning, Joe intentionally left for work without his beloved pipe. A few yards away from the house, however, Joe returned to pick up his wooden pipe from the bedroom. Looking closely at the kitchen, Joe realized that the kitchen door was wide open and that there was no trace of Jenneh on the makeshift bed where they had spent the night.

As he walked toward the bedroom, he observed that the door was locked from the inside. Joe knocked gently on the door, but got no response. In some degree of desperation, he forced the door open with a single kick. And there he found the stranger and Jenneh actively performing the act of procreation. "I knew this was going to happen," Joe angrily remarked. As he was not prepared to cause more trouble for himself that morning, however, Joe simply picked up his wooden pipe and left the room as if nothing dreadful had happened. He went to work that morning (his final working day) as usual, but with deep emotional feelings. He concentrated on his job in an attempt to take his mind off his troubles, thinking with remorse that starting tomorrow he would have to find other ways to fill his time.

After completing his day's work, Joe resisted the temptation to return directly home. Instead, he made his way to Camp Nennie to drink bamboo wine, as usual: on this occasion, not so much to induce his usual aura of relaxation, but rather to cool down his temper.

While Joe was away at work that day, both Jenneh and her pretended brother feared the inevitable consequences of the early morning drama in Joe's bedroom. The couple decided to leave that same day, without telling any of Joe's next door neighbors. The couple took every item of Joe's personal household belongings with them, including a bag of rice, a bed, drinking buckets, and cooking pots.

Joe returned home from Camp Nennie late that night only to find his house ransacked. Not only was there nothing to eat: there was no longer a bed to sleep on. He would ponder whether this was a man made curse, or something ordained by God, for the rest of his life. He paused for a while and remarked to himself, "Women appear to be the same everywhere. They may not be the evil that most men fear on Earth, but they hold the key to its dwelling place, as 'evil knows where evil sleeps.' In my book of judgment, there's hardly a faithful woman in Liberia and the rest of the world: and those who are fortunate enough to have one, did so only through divine intervention."

ELEVEN

When the chances of survival become unbearable in the ocean, as they say, "fish must eat fish."

Joe had a childhood friend in Freeman Town called Ngumbu(the (Gbandi and Mende ethnic appellation for "fire"). Joe and Ngumbu grew up in the same village in Lofa County in Liberia, but separated from each other following their graduation from the Poro initiation bush many years back. In recent years, however, they had been reunited with each other through their visits to Camp Nennie.

Although they had often met each other during such occasions, Joe had actually never called at Ngumbu's house in Freeman Town, even for a casual visit. As events unfolded in Division 80, however, Joe was obliged to visit and to seek a piece of advice from his loyal childhood friend in Freeman Town. A handsome and energetic man who had, over the years, occupied himself with subsistence swamp-rice farming in close proximity to the plantations, Ngumbu did not work for the plantation, nor did he have a wife.

In addition, his elementary educational background far exceeded the level attained by most of the clerical staff members employed by the plantations; still, many people were puzzled as to why Ngumbu made no efforts to seek employment within the company.

He had his reasons. In the early years of his arrival in the area, Ngumbu had witnessed terrible practices at the plantations. He had observed that unskilled manual laborers identified for retirement in the plantations were made to undergo strange medical tests, followed by compulsory injections, and that those who underwent such exercises died within the first six months of their retirement. Ngumbu was of the opinion that the company's compulsory medical tests and related injections were meant to shorten the lives of retirees in order to save the company from prolonged pension payments. These practices had hardened his resolve never to seek employment there.

Joe arrived in Freeman Town that morning in a somber mood. As he began to give a detailed account of what had transpired in his life, Ngumbu stood up and asked, "Have you had the compulsory retirement injection?"

Joe replied, "I haven't visited the company's health center since the day I was recruited, and I haven't taken any medical treatments from there."

Ngumbu then sat down in his hammock outside his house. Holding his wooden pipe with his left hand, he turned to Joe and said softly and slowly: "My dear friend and brother, life in this world is a gamble and at times unpredictable. You may lose a wife today, only to find another woman to marry you tomorrow. You may lose a job today, only to find another one tomorrow. But to lose your life is indeed a permanent loss. Let no one hasten you to the great beyond, which can hold great surprises. You have indeed made a wise decision not to take the Company's compulsory injection.

But you should bear in mind that the man who has destroyed your livelihood is not afraid to also destroy your natural life. And the man who destroyed your current marriage is not afraid to derail your next one: so be on your guard and remain vigilant."

As Ngumbu ended his remarks, he advised Joe to leave the company's housing unit. He offered him one of the vacant rooms in his house in Freeman Town, completely free of charge. Curiosity soon attracted an old woman in the neighborhood, who had closely followed the conversation between Ngumbu and his friend from across the street.

She briskly walked to Ngumbu's yard under the pretext of asking for tobacco to smoke in her pipe. In reality, she had come with a startling revelation. As the woman greeted Ngumbu and his friend, she revealed that a man called Mr. Gabriel Francis rented a room in her house about five years ago, for a woman called Jenneh Dao, but that a few days ago, this Mr. Francis had informed her that Jenneh's real husband had come to take her back to Lopolu and therefore no longer needed the room. After the woman made her revelation to them, she left Ngumbu and his guest to continue their normal conversation.

Although he was aware, through rumors, of the extramarital affair between his wife and Mr. Francis, Joe was certainly not aware that Jenneh was actually a married woman prior to her arrival at the plantations: she had intentionally lied to him from the beginning, for her own convenience, and had finally deceived him in the end.

As their conversation progressed, Joe could not find a better time than that very day to make the permanent move from Division 80 Housing Unit to Freeman Town, as advised by his loyal friend.

TWELVE

After Joe moved to Freeman Town, he had little appetite for food and could not sleep well most nights. He had little to tell anyone, which corresponded well with the old phrase, "Little teller tells little."

Joe would sometimes go into the bush during the day for several hours for no apparent reason. On other occasions, he would confine himself to his bedroom for the day, emerging only to attend the call of nature or when Ngumbu invited him for a meal.

This unusual behavior caused people to conclude that Joe was an extraordinary stranger with extraordinary characteristics.

It is said that a man's reflection of his past at times rekindles the fire to shape his destiny, for better or for worse. This reflective dimension was a fundamental factor in Joe's life of uncertainties. One evening Joe reflected on the memories of his early childhood. He reflected on how in his childhood, his father had given him to a dervish called Sheikh Foday Vai, for fosterage and to be taught the recitation of the Holy Quran for the purposes of Islamic worship.

Joe recalled how he had proven to be a genius under the tutorage of the sheik. He remembered how people had regarded him as the actual son of Sheikh Foday Vai, in view of his closeness and obedient servitude. Joe further reflected on how the sheik had arrived and settled in Nyandemoh-Lahun, his beloved village.

He remembered how people had perceived the sheikh to be a miraculous man who had the ability to interpret dreams, as well as to heal certain ailments such as barrenness among the women in the area. These healing skills had enhanced the sheikh's popularity. One family had offered the sheikh one of their beautiful daughters in marriage. Joe remembered how this kind gesture had persuaded the sheikh to settle in their village in order to facilitate the spiritual and healing needs of the people of Nyandemoh-Lahun.

And Joe remembered how in later years, the sheikh was able to marry three more wives in succession, thus making him a man of four wives in his own right. Joe's Islamic education had abruptly come to an end when the sheikh decided to permanently return home to his native Vai homeland.

Joe further remembered how the sheikh had told the people of Nyandemoh-Lahun one evening of his final departure that now that he had his own biological children to take care of, he could no longer care for a foster child like Joe. The sheikh left Nyandemoh-Lahun, which effectively ended all sources of communication between him and the rest of the local people in the village.

In his new found distress, Joe thought that if the sheikh were still alive, then it was necessary for him to go and look for him. If he were still the same type of man he had known in his childhood, Joe was convinced that the sheikh would be able to find a lasting solution to his problems through spiritual invocation.

Joe one morning anxiously waited on the Freeman Town–Monrovia highway, where he got a ride with the first vehicle that came by. As the vehicle arrived in Monrovia, Liberia's capital city, Joe got into another vehicle bound for Grand Capemount County, the original home of the sheikh. Joe's journey was however delayed by an interesting drama.

From the waterfront parking station in Monrovia, the driver drove slowly and crossed the Boatswain Bridge linking greater Monrovia with Cassava Island, two sections of the same city. In the interest of his passengers, the driver had chosen this route mainly to evade a notorious time- and money-consuming police checkpoint.

But halfway onto Cassava Island, all traffic came to a dead halt. People were running from all directions toward the city's most popular nightclub, known as "the Jungle." Behind the Jungle stood a man in a three-piece brown suit, profusely perspiring in the dry Harmattan weather blowing in from the Sahara, and wiping his face with a white handkerchief.

The man did not say his name, but judging from his appearance, one could easily guess his social status in the community: he was a "big shot."

Curious to find out what the commotion was, the passengers in the vehicle started to get out one by one. Joe, who from childhood was unaccustomed to telling hearsay stories when he could provide a first-hand account, decided to see for himself what was afoot. He went directly toward the crowd, holding his old raffia bag tightly to ensure that it wouldn't be snatched by the thieves who typically took advantage of such chaotic situations to rob travelers.

In front of him stood a tall bald man questioning a middle-aged man who was neatly dressed in traditional regalia.

"Where is the occupant of that house?" the bald man asked.

"I don't know for certain," replied the middle-aged man.

"And when do you think he'll be back?" the bald man further inquired.

"I do not know for sure. All I can say is that the man who lives in that house paid me the full twelve-month rent on the same day he moved in."

Out of the crowd came an inquisitive old lady with a walking stick. She struggled to reach the landlord of the property in question to let him know that during the early hours of the morning, she had seen a group of three men approached the missing man in question, and picked up three heavy-looking suitcases to a nearby parked car. She had overheard the man telling the driver, "Abidjan, and quickly."

Upon hearing the statement from the old woman, the bald man in the brown suit collapsed and fell to the ground, hitting his head hard on the concrete next to Joe's left foot.

As the surrounding onlookers panicked, paramedics were called to the scene and upon arrival saw white foam running out of the man's mouth.

In his curiosity to know the full story of the occupant of the house behind the nightclub and why the man in the brown suit had collapsed, Joe spoke to the old woman. Before she could reply, the woman asked whether Joe could understand the Vai tribal language, as she didn't want many people to hear what she was about to say.

When Joe replied that he only spoke "simple Liberian English," she gave a little smile and told Joe that the man who had gone off to Abidjan was a "money doubler." In recent weeks he had performed numerous miracles in the presence of many people in Monrovia and convinced them that if one gave him one hundred US dollars, that person, in return, was sure to find a thousand dollars within twenty-four hours under his or her pillowcase. The brown-suit man, along with several senior government officials, had given the money doubler thousands of dollars with the hope of becoming overnight millionaires. This had yet to happen, but the miracle man had now gone off with the money he had collected.

Upon hearing the story behind the event, Joe made his way back to the vehicle to join the other passengers, who were already scrambling for better seats. He was the last passenger to get into the vehicle and had to squeeze himself into the small back seat, normally reserved for the apprentice, locally referred to as a "car boy."

The traffic had by now become less congested and the driver resumed the journey, which by now was two hours behind schedule.

Joe arrived in the first village in which he thought the sheikh might be found. As he emerged from the vehicle, Joe went to the first house to ask for Sheik Foday Vai, but the people there said they knew no one by such a name.

Joe went to a second house, where the occupants told him the same thing. He then went to three more houses and got similar responses. In sheer exasperation, Joe finally requested the occupants of the fifth house to direct him to the town chief. He knew by tradition that it was always the responsibility of a town chief to provide strangers with food and a place to sleep in cases where no relatives could be found to provide such hospitality.

As he pondered the discouraging impression he'd received in the first village, a little boy volunteered to take Joe to the town chief. Before the boy could do so, however, curiosity soon drew the attention of a blind man who had overheard the conversation between the stranger and the occupants of the fifth house.

The blind man twice cleared his throat and inquired about what the stranger wanted. Joe walked over to him and explained that he had come to look for a religious man by the name of Sheikh Foday Vai, who had once been his tutor.

The blind man sat speechless for a while, during which time Joe thought their brief conversation had ended. He was just about to leave when the blind man once again spoke: "Sheikh Foday Vai once lived here with a large family. But a few years later he moved from here; no one knows why. You will probably never find him by his real name."

"Why is that?" Joe asked.

"He is now known throughout the Vai country as Kai-Kpanda, which means 'for Nothing Man,' in case you don't know." "I am not too sure where he might be at the moment, but he used to stay in a little hamlet called Dar-es-Salaam, which is a stone's throw from here. You will probably find him there if you ask for Kai-Kpanda instead of Sheikh Foday Vai," said the blind man.

"But why did he change his name?" Joe asked again, curious.

The blind man gave a little smile and again cleared his throat. "Sheikh Foday Vai, as he was once called, arrived here many years ago with four wives and many children. But just when everyone thought that all was well with him and his family, a tragedy struck: he became impotent. Within a matter of months, all of his wives had deserted him except the senior wife who, for one reason or another, decided to stay with him until death would part them. The news of his impotency quickly spread like wildfire. Since then, women in this region have referred to him as 'Kai-Kpanda' because he is incapable of taking a woman to bed."

What a terrible news! Tired, weak, and worn, Joe began to tremble in disbelief as he heard the unfortunate circumstances about his former tutor.

It was getting late when he once again requested the occupants in the fifth house for directions to Dar-es-Salaam, which he knew meant "Haven of Peace." He was told it was not far away.

As Joe arrived in the little hamlet, he soon discovered that Kai-Kpanda had moved out some years back, to settle in a much larger village not far from Dar-es-Salaam. He had to make another trek through the countryside. He arrived at the sheikh's new village just before sunset. As he approached the first house and asked for Kai-Kpanda, a young lady pointed to a new thatched-roof mud house.

Joe walked there quickly and met an old man smoking his pipe on the veranda of the house, lying in a hammock. He greeted the old man, who acknowledged his greeting. Joe was not sure whether this old man was the right person he had suffered so much to look for. He was obliged to ask him directly, "Old man, are you Sheikh Foday Vai?"

The sheikh took a keen look at Joe before he acknowledged that he was.

"My name is Joe Blackee; do you still remember me?" Joe asked.

The old man instantly remembered the familiar name and got out of his hammock with tears in his eyes. The two men embraced each other with great emotion, after which the old man shouted for his loyal senior wife, Hawa, to come and meet their new guest.

Hawa promptly came and embraced Joe with great joy as she too remembered his name. She rushed into the kitchen to bring a red rooster for her husband to slaughter so that she could prepare a proper meal for the stranger. The cooking was intermittently interrupted by a series of questions and answers from both the sheikh and his wife, and from Joe, after years of separation.

While the cooking progressed, Hawa took a bucket of hot water to a nearby makeshift bathroom at the back of the house and requested that the stranger have his evening bath.

As the food was readied, Joe sat to eat the evening meal in the company of his hosts. Joe then offered a symbolic token of greetings: a white dollar coin, a heap of tobacco, and two wooden pipes. Joe knew from his childhood that his hosts were once habitual tobacco smokers. He then offered the couple a bar of his once-beloved oil palm plantation blue washing soap.

The sheikh heartily received the stranger's kind gesture and spoke: "A bird never misses its nest; nor does a river change its course of flowing. Whatever kindness a man does on Earth will one day be rewarded, either in this life or in the hereafter. I knew that one day you would come and look for me no matter what the circumstances would be, and that is exactly what you've done today."

Already armed with the full story of Sheikh Foday's "social" ailment, as narrated by the blind old man, Joe refrained from asking further questions about the whereabouts of the sheikh's other three wives. Instead, he limited his conversation to an explanation of the purpose of his own visit.

Joe began with an account of what had transpired in his personal life in the Oil Palm Plantations Company, with tears running down both cheeks. He ended with how his immediate boss in the plantations had brought about his early retirement, as well as disrupting his five-year marriage to Jenneh.

The sheikh very much regretted the unfortunate events that had befallen his former pupil. He rose to his feet and slowly went to his bedroom. He reemerged with the wooden pipe presented to him earlier by Joe, along with a piece of tobacco that he rolled and placed within it. Walking toward the fire hearth in the kitchen, the sheikh lit the pipe and began to smoke. He swiftly returned and sat in his hammock with the pipe in his mouth. He then held Joe's right hand and asked, "What do you intend to do next?"

"I want to get revenge by whatever means—not necessarily to get my wife and my job back, but to stop those in higher positions from breaking innocent people's marriages under the protection of juju-men," said Joe.

"Do you know the home of Jenneh?" The sheikh further asked.

"She and my former boss, Gabriel Francis, both hail from Lopolu," replied Joe.

He remembered how as a young man, he had once briefly settled in Lopolu. He took a deep breath and again asked Joe, in a slow, deep voice: "Do you know about the people of Lopolu?"

"No, not precisely, but I'm told it's one of the most dangerous juju-oriented areas of this country."

Sheikh Foday got up and looked toward the sky. He reflected on his past memories.

The sheikh looked toward the sky again and firmly held Joe's hands. "To go to Lopolu—and most importantly, to seek vengeance on anyone there—is a dangerous venture. You must be properly protected against the powers of juju, witchcraft, and other malevolent forces. Unfortunately, I do not possess such instruments of protection. But there may be other avenues to explore. As it is already late, we cannot say and do everything tonight, however. Instead, let's sleep on the issue until daybreak."

Joe agreed to what the sheikh had suggested; later that night he was given a comfortable bedroom in which to spend the night. He enjoyed a sound sleep for the first time since his enforced retirement from the Oil Palm Plantations Company.

By daybreak the next morning, Joe brought up the issue raised by the sheikh the previous night, in which the old man suggested seeking help elsewhere. Sheikh Foday took Joe aside for a confidential chat; he reemphasized the need to consult a fortune-teller.

"But where can we find such a person?" Joe asked. "These days, many fortune-tellers are nothing more than crooks, bent on making quick money by lying to their clients."

Sheikh Foday informed Joe of a man in the nearby village, whose name was Samuka. He indicated that Samuka was a highly respected "factual" fortune-teller with a great reputation.

"How do you know he told the truth?" Joe asked, somewhat skeptical.

Sheikh Foday rebuked him for making such a remark about the man in question. He went on to give numerous demonstrations of Samuka's credibility in the art of factual fortune-telling. He began by telling of how Samuka had once predicted that the only daughter of the commissioner of Wakor, the regional capital of the Vai country, was doomed to be killed by a crocodile.

The sheikh explained that the commissioner, as a precautionary measure, had ordered the construction of a four-story building to house his only daughter on the building's highest floor. In spite of this precaution, the commissioner's daughter became obsessed with looking at various species of live fish brought in by her mother's attendants immediately after each fishing event, which were commonly held events in that region. In true testimony of Samuka's prediction, one of the baskets brought to the commissioner's daughter for viewing contained a baby crocodile.

As the young woman put her hand into the fishing basket to view its contents, she apparently touched the tail of the baby crocodile, which bit her on the tip of the finger. She immediately dropped the little reptile back into the basket without saying a word.

Quite unknown to the woman who had brought the basket, the commissioner's daughter soon developed a swollen finger. In spite of all the medical facilities available to the commissioner's household, his only daughter died that same night.

Sheikh Foday Vai ended his defense of the fortune-teller with a second example, explaining to Joe how it had been revealed to Samuka himself in a dream that one of his junior wives was having an illicit affair with a famous fisherman in the village. The sheikh explained how one morning, Samuka had requested the wife in question to confess to the act. Because she refused to do so, Samuka predicted that the man in question would be drowned within seven days. As it came to pass, the man's remains were found floating in the fisherman's lake, now called Lake Pisso, precisely seven days later, just as Samuka had predicted.

Now convinced by the sheikh's words, Joe urged him to take him to Samuka without delay.

THIRTEEN

Joe had spent a sleepless night contemplating the outcome of his impending visit to Samuka and what sort of action he should take to avenge the loss of his home, his wife, and above all, his livelihood in the oil palm plantations.

The next morning Joe and his host departed to visit Samuka in another village, just a few miles away. When they arrived, they met up with Samuka, who was just returning from his early morning prayers at the mosque. They greeted each other in typical Vai tradition.

"What has brought you here early this morning?" Samuka inquired.

"If you see a tortoise running for cover in the middle of the day, there is fire on its back," Sheikh Foday remarked proverbially.

Without further ado, Samuka took his guests to the veranda of his round thatched-roof hut, located in the center of the village, where, as expected, many other people were already waiting to consult the great fortune-teller. Following an exchange of jokes, Samuka asked Sheikh Foday to fully explain the purpose of their visit.

"My son here has been badly treated by his enemies. He intends to exact revenge on those who caused trouble for him. He intends to go to a place he has never been before. He therefore wants to know, through your sooth-saying skills, if his journey will be successful or not."

Samuka entered his bedroom, invited his guests in, and offered them seats. He looked under his bed and took out an old, black, tainted book. Samuka gently opened the book and took out a plain sheet of paper. The fortune-teller again looked under the bed and brought out a little ink container, along with a long eagle's feather, which he used as a pen to write and to conduct his divine consultations.

As Samuka began his shamanistic consultation, he dipped the pointed edge of the feather into the ink container with his right hand and started to make several dots on the blank sheet of paper. The dots were placed in rows of one, three, five, seven, and nine. He then carefully tallied the number of dots in each row before writing the totals in Arabic.

As Samuka completed his rituals of writing and counting, he gently placed the white sheet of paper (now partly covered with dots) and its totals aside, and reached out for his guidebook for possible predictions. He then placed the book of predictions on his right leg in normal prayer position on the mat and carefully looked at each recorded total of dots and compared his analysis with the guidebook.

Samuka cautiously closed the guidebook and placed the paper he had used in the same black book from where it had previously been removed. He then placed all of the items back in their normal places as if there were nothing more to be said or done. He then cleared his throat twice and turned toward his guests. "The place your son intends to go is full of juju and men with bad intentions. He will probably get what he wants from there if he uses his intelligence prudently. If your son had ever gone there, the people of that village would put him to a trivial test to prove if he was the person he professed to be. Upon arrival, he will be given a room in a house where many other families live. Before bedtime, the occupants of that house will begin to move out one by one with their belongings. He should be vigilant to also get out of the house immediately after the last people have moved out. He should wait in the bush to see what follows next."

"The following morning, he will probably be able to accomplish his mission better than he can possibly imagine. I must warn him, however, not to spend the second night in that village if he survives the first night."

"He should also remember that lime is traditionally a powerful device against the strengths of juju. He must carry lime on his body for this reason and make sure to rub himself with the juice before his arrival in the village. Your son should also refrain from shaking hands with people in that village. If he ever does so, it will be his last handshake in this life."

"Most importantly, your son will be offered food and alcoholic drink under the pretext of good hospitality. While the food will be safe to eat, the alcoholic drink will be a deadly poison."

As Samuka concluded his divine predictions, he bade farewell to his guests in order to make room for other people who had been waiting.

FOURTEEN

Seven days had passed since Joe first found Sheikh Foday Vai and his wife. On the evening of that seventh day, he begged leave of the sheikh and his wife to return to Freeman Town. On the morning of Joe's departure, the sheikh recited specially selected verses of the Holy Quran and invoked Allah's blessings upon his beloved former pupil.

He asked Allah to protect Joe against the evil forces of the people of Lopolu and to spare his life so that he may return home safely. With these spiritual invocations, Joe and the sheikh, along with his wife, embraced each other, after which Joe assured them that he would visit them regularly in the near future, provided he returned safely from Lopolu. Joe left the Vai region that morning, full of hope and determination.

As Joe arrived in Monrovia en route to Freeman Town, he decided to take a stroll around the perimeter of the city's waterfront in an attempt to kill time before continuing on to his final destination. As he did so, he saw three boys running toward the Boatswain Bridge, not far from where he stood. Behind them was an old man crying for help, for reasons unknown to Joe. Within minutes, the boys had vanished in the direction of the notorious district known as "Bend-Down Corner," the "no-go" area for the police in Monrovia.

This event troubled Joe. He wondered why, given that the waterfront area was crowded with a multitude of traders and ordinary people, not a single person had come forward to intercept the thieves. Joe observed that two fundamental factors were responsible for this: first, the boys were known to many traders in the waterfront market as dangerous gangsters who knifed people who stood in their way when fleeing their unsavory activities. Second, they were infamous for the inevitable violent revenge they exacted on those who identified them to the metropolitan police. For these reasons, no one ever dared to interfere whenever there was a shout of "Thieves!" in the waterfront parking station.

The old man's traditional regalia told Joe that he was of the Kpelleh ethnic group, the largest in Liberia. Joe walked toward the victim in an attempt to find out what happened. With tears running from both eyes, the old man said, "I came all the way from Gbakokoyata, in the heartland of the Kpelleh country, to buy some zinc to roof my seven-bedroom mud house to accommodate my six wives and twelve children."

"I brought two hundred dollars with me, which I obtained from the local Cooperative Club as a loan. While I was visiting the stores on the waterfront, a young man approached and asked me in my own Kpelleh dialect what I was looking for, and trusting him for this reason, I told him that I was looking for 'six bundles of zinc.'"

"He told me that he would help me purchase up to ten bundles of high-quality zinc, but wanted to know how much money I had first. I told him that I had two hundred dollars. The young man then told me to wait while he went to make arrangements to have the zinc brought to the parking station. He returned a few minutes later with two other friends—but without the zinc. They demanded the payment. When I asked how much, one of them told me: 'one hundred and forty dollars.' While I was counting the money from my wallet, one of them snatched the money from me, and the three of them ran off with everything I had with me."

As the old man concluded his explanation of what had transpired, Joe generously offered him a handsome gift to facilitate his journey back to his village. He gently placed his hand on the old man's shoulder and said, "This is Monrovia, and telling a strange person you've never met about how much money you have is like leaving a heap of cassava leaves near a hungry goat, while you went to the bush to attend to nature. Would you really expect to find the cassava leaves still there upon your return? No! Never! Let this be a lesson to you from now on!"

FIFTEEN

Joe's multilingual fluency allowed him to freely travel anywhere in Liberia without obstacles. On this occasion, the Gola language spoken by most of the people of Lopolu posed no problem to him.

Joe had left Freeman Town en route to Lopolu on a special mission. He had suffered enough at the hands of Jenneh Dao and Gabriel Francis, who both hailed from Lopolu. They had caused him to lose everything he had worked for in his life in the plantations and therefore deserved to be punished. And the juju-men who had protected them must equally be punished, by hook or by crook.

Joe didn't know the route from Freeman to Lopolu for certain. He had never been there and had only heard by word of mouth about a major footpath that extended from the Gola forests to a village called Zuehn, located in close proximity of Lopolu.

Determination is the key to success, and with all human instincts, determination knows no fear: and Joe's thirst to punish his archenemies in Lopolu remained unquenchable. Joe spent several days and nights trekking under perilous circumstances to find his way to Lopolu.

He had run out of provisions by the second day of his journey, and only by sheer good luck did he come across a pawpaw tree with ripe fruits in a fallow land near an abandoned well. There, he regained his strength after eating the fruits and drinking a good quantity of water. He continued his journey.

And as the sun was about to set, Joe came across a lone man who received him in a friendly—albeit somewhat suspicious—manner. The man had lived alone in the forest for over two decades, and during those years had never seen any traveler coming his way.

The hermit offered Joe freshly tapped bamboo wine and shared his evening meal with him. During their meal, the man inquired about where Joe was heading, to which he replied, "Lopolu." The mention of the town raised an eyebrow for the man, who became speechless for a while. Since he didn't hear a word from him, Joe broke the silence by asking what was amiss. The hermit put aside what he was eating to address his guest's question.

He began to tell Joe how he had once lived in Lopolu during his youth, where he had built a zinc-roofed house, married, and had four children. In the years that followed, he soon realized that the people of Lopolu generally did not like strangers to dwell in their midst on a permanent basis, regardless of ethnicity.

He explained to Joe how one hot afternoon he had gone to take a bath in the Lopo River, the river after which Lopolu was named. But before he could even take off his garments, a multitude of bees mysteriously appeared and attacked him with such severe intensity that he had to jump into the river head-first to drive the bees away.

As he emerged from the river, he observed that the bees had mysteriously disappeared in the same manner in which they had appeared to attack him. That was not the end of the matter, the hermit said. As he returned to the village after the encounter with the bees, he found that his house was ablaze, and within minutes it was reduced to ashes. He found no trace of his wife and children. All efforts to gather information about his wife and children proved futile, as people refused to talk to him.

He decided to leave Lopolu immediately and had since remained in his secluded lowly hut, deep in the forest. Joe was the first person ever to have come across him in the forest. As the lonely man concluded his remarks, Joe reflected on what he'd been told about the people of Lopolu by Samuka the fortune-teller. As the hut had two rooms, Joe was given the spare room in which to spend the night.

The following morning, the hermit gave Joe precise directions to Lopolu, but warned him of the inevitable dangers that awaited strangers there.

After leaving the hermit's abode, it didn't take long for Joe to come across an old man bound by rope and tied to a cotton tree deep in the forest. Joe attempted to ease the old man's suffering, but his offer of help was met with defiance. The man said, "Why don't you mind your own business and just leave me alone?"

Joe insisted on knowing why the old man was bound by rope and left alone in the forest. The man relented and told him that he was of the Gola tribe and that his fate was like the fate of every Gola man, as was ordained by Daya at the time of creation. As Joe heard this story, he left the old man alone, bound by rope to await his inevitable fate in the forest.

After four days on the road, Joe finally arrived one Thursday evening at the bank of the Lopo River, not far from Lopolu. Heeding the stories narrated by the hermit in the forest and the warnings by Samuka the fortune-teller, Joe decided not to enter Lopolu itself that evening.

Instead, he decided to spend the night in the trunk of an old cotton tree that stood above the river. From his vantage point, Joe began to observe the ritual bath differences between high-ranking juju priests and ordinary men.

He observed that the juju-men wore no footwear at all and that these juju-men wore red hats with three lines of cowry shells running parallel to each side of their heads. They put their hats aside at the bank of the river before entering the water.

He also observed that the high-ranking juju-men first placed their left legs into the water before the right ones. Following a series of observations, Joe waited until the last man had left the riverside, at which time he emerged to have his own cold bath. He then returned to his hiding place for the rest of the night.

SIXTEEN

Strange arrival can often be met with strange reception, and like a strange fish in an unfamiliar river, the swimming may take an unfamiliar course.

Joe left his hiding place the next morning and made his way to the heart of Lopolu. There, he intermingled with various traders and had good conversations with many in the open market, although he never revealed his name or true identity to anyone. By late afternoon, as traders began to leave for their homes, Joe made a quick exit from the market and went into the nearby forest. There, he rubbed his entire body with lime juice, as advised by the fortune-teller. He then put on his traditional regalia: black shorts, black T-shirt, and black hat, nicely decorated with three lines of cowry shells, traditionally known in Liberia as "Gamble."

Joe's decorated items were in the form of a cross running from the back of his head to the front and from the right ear to the left. He also had a horsetail that he had obtained en route to Lopolu. Holding the horsetail with his right hand, Joe made his way to the center of town.

Joe's appearance as a stranger in the market soon attracted the attention of a great crowd of people. Women and children began clapping their hands, expecting Joe to raise a song, which was the habit of insane people who passed by on open market days in Lopolu. Their clapping continued, but the women and children were disappointed when Joe didn't raise any song. Instead, he continued his intended activity. The crowd followed him wherever he went. As Joe approached a large hut, which he rightly guessed to be the town hall, he abruptly stopped. In a sharp voice, he asked, who is the chief of this town?

The clapping of the women and children suddenly ceased. A half-naked man soon charged forward from the crowd to inquire what was amiss.

"I want to speak directly to the chief of this town," Joe insisted.

The man led Joe to the chief's compound, and the crowd followed. Before the man could introduce the stranger, however, Joe performed a strange ritual in front of the curious crowd. He went around the hut four times and hit the ground four times with the horsetail in his right hand, followed by whispering strange words to himself.

The chief of Lopolu, who had observed the proceedings from his veranda, got out of his hammock. He looked on with curiosity, as both the stranger's appearance and the rituals he performed were a bit out of the ordinary. The chief did not ask for the stranger's name, nor where he had come from. The stranger, in turn, didn't disclose his name.

One man in the crowd whispered to a nearby friend in Mandingo to let the chief know that the stranger was insane. Joe apparently overheard and understood the man's statement; he promptly responded in perfect Mandingo that he was a sane man who had come to Lopolu on a special mission.

A moment later, another man openly remarked, speaking in the Kpelleh language: "every Friday we receive a lunatic in the open market, but this one is the funniest of all."

Again, Joe responded in perfect Kpelleh: "Among the lunatics you've seen in your open market in the past, I am going to be the last your eyes shall ever see. For when I leave tomorrow, you'll never see one insane person in your market again for the rest of your natural lives."

Within moments of his arrival, Joe had spoken nearly every tribal language known to the people of Lopolu. This linguistic ability finally convinced the chief that the man in their midst that night was an extraordinary stranger with unpredictable attributes.

Joe then made a traditional offer of a white coin to the chief as a token of greetings to the people of Lopolu, which was accepted as a symbolic gesture. A moment later, the chief ordered the town crier to summon every denizen of Lopolu to assemble in the veranda of his compound, which was promptly done. Within minutes, the chief's compound was full to capacity, and there began a series of whispering and exchange of words between the chief, his councilmen, and the senior elders of Lopolu, about the stranger.

A few moments after the gathering, the chief and his councilmen walked out of the veranda, without an explanation to Joe or to the audience, to a secluded area completely out of the stranger's view, for a closed-door consultation. Following a brief deliberation, the men returned to the veranda with an array of items, which they presented to Joe as a welcoming present.

The items included a split red kola nut and ground green pepper, crowned with a pinch of salt and a drop of edible red palm oil.

Joe carefully observed the unusual items with both concern and suspicion. Being a traditionalist who knew the tribal rituals of Liberia, Joe at once understood exactly what the items symbolized. To him, a kola nut with pepper and salt symbolized purity of heart, while a mixture of red palm oil added to such items symbolized eminent danger of a ritualistic nature, with far-reaching consequences for the person involved. With this in mind, Joe received the array of items in the tray with his left hand and placed it on the floor.

To the people of Lopolu, this was culturally not a gesture of appreciation, but rather was an insult to the host community. The chief, realizing that the stranger was not, after all, ignorant of the customs of his village, rose to his feet and remarked, "Every token of greeting from a stranger is always accompanied by a message. What message do you have to tell the people of Lopolu tonight?"

Joe twice hit the arm of the chair with his right hand to alert the people to pay heed to what he was about to say. He then gave a little smile before he stood up to his full height. He waved the horsetail twice over both shoulders. Joe looked to both sides of the veranda and bowed his head in reverence. He diligently charged forward into the middle of the veranda without saying a word. There, he stood with arms akimbo and said, "I'm the supreme head of all the juju-men in Liberia and beyond. I have been commanded by the spirits of my ancestors to visit every community throughout the length and breadth of Liberia to purify both malign and benign medicines of a ritualistic nature. I never intended to come to your village."

"But a few months ago, the spirits of my ancestors appealed to me in a vision that unless I visited Lopolu to purify both men and women involved with the practice of juju, there would be no peace for the rest of my life."

"I had ignored such calls until three nights ago, when I was given a final stern warning that there was only one step between me and death if I did not obey their commands. It is for fear of my own life and for the sake of the people of Lopolu that I have made my way to this ancient village tonight. I must warn everyone gathered here that their failure to surrender their juju items to me by sunrise tomorrow for purification will result in their juju paraphernalia not only becoming dysfunctional, but also in their owners becoming insane."

The chief became furious over the stranger's threat against his village. At first he refused to have further dealings with Joe, but later changed his mind. He then passed the matter over to the senior elders of Lopolu. There began a murmur of low and loud voices.

In view of the stranger's mention of juju, the town chief specifically referred the matter to the most senior juju-man of Lopolu, called Gotola. Gotola rose to his feet and came forward. He offered a handshake to the stranger, but this gesture was rejected by Joe.

Offended by the stranger's action, Gotola retreated to his seat. The chief of Lopolu then asked Gotola what should be done in response to the stranger's demands. Before the chief could finish what he was saying, however, one elderly man among the crowd shouted in the Lorma language that "only a fool can obey such order."

Prompt action with prompt reaction. Joe told the man in perfect Lorma that "such a fool, ready to obey my order, would be the only survivor in the village after my departure from here tomorrow."

The man who made the remark couldn't wait to leave the venue after hearing the stranger speaking in perfect Lorma. Another senior elder who was aggrieved by the stranger's threatening behavior told the chief to let the stranger leave the village at once. But the chief rebuked him, saying, "It is our avowed ancient custom never to drive a stranger from our village under the cover of darkness; that tradition cannot be changed under any circumstances."

The other elders nodded in acknowledgement of what their chief had said. Gotola came closer to the chief and whispered a word in his right ear. The chief nodded his head twice in agreement. He then turned to the stranger and said, "We'll respond to your mandate early in the morning, but for now, we will only welcome you to our village and give you a place to sleep."

Following the meeting, the chief of Lopolu left the venue without further discussion with the stranger. The acrimonious meeting with the chief and elders was followed by a certain degree of hospitality. A woman brought a bucket of water for the stranger to have his evening bath before the meal was ready, but the stranger informed her that he had already had his cold bath before arriving in the village.

A moment later, the chief's senior wife brought Joe a well-prepared meal in a tray, along with drinking water and a wooden spoon. Joe greedily ate the food until he was full. While he ate, the chief, who had earlier left the veranda, returned with palm wine in a gourd to give to the stranger. Joe thanked the chief for his kind gesture, but politely remarked that palm wine was his taboo. To Joe's surprise, the chief angrily threw the gourd of palm wine away. It hit one of the pillars of the hut and broke into so many pieces that its contents spilled all over the veranda.

It wasn't long before the chief requested Joe to follow him. From the town hall, he led Joe to an extraordinary house at the center of Lopolu: a five-bedroom mud house with a zinc roof.

One room in particular was well-furnished, and Joe was told to spend the night there. While the stranger was inspecting the room, the chief left without a final goodnight to his guest.

The families occupying the other four bedrooms of the house started leaving for other houses with their belongings on their heads. Joe promptly remembered what Samuka the fortune-teller had predicted. Plagued by fear, Joe waited until the last families had left the house, after which he, too, immediately got out of the room and took refuge in a goat shed at the outskirts of the village.

In the middle of the night, without any sign of rain, a terrible stroke of lightning struck the five-bedroom house. It was set ablaze and was reduced to ashes within minutes.

Although this event lasted for a brief period, it did create quite a noise; despite this, not a single person came out to see what had happened, let alone to ask if the stranger had survived. Joe used the occasion to his advantage. He emerged from the goat shed early the next morning and made his way to the ashes of the burned-down house.

It was still a somewhat dark when Joe arrived on the scene, and he looked on both sides of the burnt house to make sure that no one had observed where he had been, or what he was about to do. He lay flat on his stomach in the ashes at the precise location of the room that he had been given the previous night.

Unaware that the stranger had survived the terrible ordeal, two women, on their way to the river to fetch water early that morning, saw Joe in the ashes with his clothing intact. The women fled at once, but before they could run away, Joe rose to his feet from the ashes and ordered them to stop.

He firmly instructed the two women: "Go and tell your chief that what happened here last night was just an example of what is yet to come. If his people refused to surrender their juju items to me this morning, there will be tears and mourning in every household after my departure. Their juju activities will be an event of the past: insanity and death shall be their reward."

As the two women ran to reveal their discovery to their chief and their fellow villagers, the chief and his senior juju-man of Lopolu were the first to rush to the scene to see for themselves what had transpired overnight. The town crier couldn't wait to be told to relay the message. Beating an empty tortoise shell, he urged the people of Lopolu to bring all juju paraphernalia in their possession to the stranger for ritual purification, which had an immediate effect. Within moments, there was a long line of men and women who scrambled to surrender whatever juju implements were in their possession.

As they surrendered their juju items to him, the stranger ordered each person to explain, in detail, the functions of each item surrendered, the type of herbs used in its preparation, and the cultural norms and taboos regarding its use. One by one, each person narrated the functions of their juju paraphernalia, in order of their power.

Then came one of the moments Joe had not expected, but it produced one of his greatest triumphs: an old woman known only as "Mother Healer" stepped forward with six rolls of white chalk, mixed with various herbs. She told the stranger that although she was not a juju practitioner, she was a common herbalist who healed men suffering from impotency. Joe smiled and looked at the woman with admiration and anxiety, and then he asked, "How do you treat your patients?"

The old woman replied, "Each man with the ailment is to dissolve at least half a roll of the chalk in a cup of water, then add a pinch of table salt to it. He should drink the herbs at least three times a day. He should repeat the process for at least four days, after which he should discontinue. If he is someone with ordinary genital impotency or that caused by juju or witchcraft, he will immediately regain his genital potency during the first few days of the treatment. But if it was something natural, he will never be cured."

As Mother Healer concluded her remarks, Joe told her, "Certainly, these items do not need to be purified, as they are meant to heal people. I will, however, take with me what you've brought here. All you need to do is to tell me the type of herbs you normally use in their preparation."

In fear of the stranger's powers, she called the names of several herbs already known to Joe, but who did not know their healing potential. Mother Healer then showed Joe the chemistry of how to prepare the mixture of herbs in a wooden mortar with a lump of white clay.

Proud and satisfied with his achievement, the stranger finally told the people of Lopolu that he was going away into the bush for seven days and seven nights, during which time their juju items would be purified and promptly returned to their rightful owners.

Joe warned the people that during those seven days he was away in the bush, no one was to leave Lopolu under any circumstances until he returned, and that anyone who did otherwise, and tried to follow or spy on him, would drop dead on the very spot from where he or she was spying.

After accomplishing his mission, Joe left Lopolu with an array of juju items in a loaded sack on his head and made his way back to Freeman Town, unbeknownst to the people. For the requisite seven days and seven nights, the people of Lopolu were left in limbo, for Joe had effectively put an end to all their juju activities by taking every item of juju paraphernalia with him for his own personal use.

From that time forward, it became a tradition that any stranger who came to Lopolu dressed in black regalia should be greeted with a hail of stones to hasten his departure.

SEVENTEEN

The virtues of healing and fortune-telling, as arts of divine medium, were skills a man or a woman must possess to attain social respect and popularity among indigenous populations of Liberia. The value of "native doctors" was therefore highly recognized in Liberia, which was why the Ministry of the Interior had a special branch that was responsible for the monitoring, supervision, and licensing of people who served as native doctors.

As Joe became aware that his newly acquired juju skills effectively fell within the realm of native doctors, he decided to visit the interior ministry on Camp Johnson Road in Monrovia to obtain a legally recognized license. This would allow him to practice without violating the law. Upon arrival at the interior ministry, a clerical staff woman led Joe into the crowded office of one Mr. Gordon Gordonson, popularly known as "GG" for short.

GG was the Director of Traditional Medicines and Cultural Practices, a position he had held for over forty years. The clerk briefly explained the purpose of Joe's mission to GG; it didn't take long for Joe to realize that at the interior ministry, the processing of documents largely depended on the financial contribution one was prepared to offer: the higher the amount offered, the faster the process.

GG turned to Joe after a few moments and asked, "How many miles have you traveled to come here?"

Joe was puzzled at first, about both the simplicity and complexity of the question, as he was not familiar with the customs of the interior ministry; he could not give a definitive answer. Joe began to scratch his head. The woman who'd shown him in, who knew the answer to such enigmas, took him aside and said, "When GG asked about how many miles you have traveled to come to Monrovia, he was referring to how much money you've brought as his 'cold water,' in addition to the forty dollars required as the official license fee."

Joe turned his back to the clerk to protect his privacy while getting out his wallet. He counted seventy-five dollars in cash and handed it over to the clerk, who then shouted to GG at the top of her sharp voice: "Seventy-five miles, sir"!

This was not the end of the matter. After receiving the money, GG again asked Joe, "What proof do you have to convince me that you're a qualified native doctor?"

Joe was taken aback. He wondered why GG had not considered the issue of qualification before receiving the license fee. He rose from his seat and went to the entrance door. There, Joe looked to both sides of the corridor and asked the office clerk, where can I find the men's room?

"The men's room is on the left side of GG's office," replied the clerk.

On his way to the men's room, Joe whispered something to himself. As he entered the bathroom, there appeared a large python under the desk of GG, with a white chicken half-swallowed in its mouth.

GG's secretary was the first person to see the snake curled up close to her boss's right foot. In a panic, she dropped the glass of cold water meant for a nearby thirsty visitor. She rushed out of the office, loudly shouting for GG to leave at once, as there was a large snake under his desk. When GG spotted the snake under his desk, he immediately jumped to his feet and left the office. In the process, he stumbled twice but did not fall. When GG finally got out of his office, everyone could see the wetness of his trousers from the upper legs down to the soles of his feet. Whether this was the result of the water spilled out of the glass dropped by his secretary or that of his own urine (or a combination of both) was anyone's guess. One thing was for certain: GG looked terribly shaken.

Joe calmly emerged from the men's room, completely unconcerned about the issue of the snake, and slowly walked back to GG's office. Joe sat in the same chair facing GG's desk where he had sat before going to the men's room. From his vantage point, Joe observed the ensuing pandemonium around the premises of the interior ministry. People were rushing to get hold of crowbars and machetes to kill the snake. Before long, the municipal police were on the spot to help kill the creature. The police officers, unaware of the complexity of the issue at hand, decided to follow their normal official routine, which was to inspect the scene of the incident before taking any action.

To their surprise, they found Joe sitting in the same location where the snake was reported to have been spotted.

"Get out of that office at once!" shouted one of the police officers, holding a single-barrel gun in his hands. "That snake has to be shot dead," the officer further remarked.

The preliminary findings of the police confirmed that there was no snake to be seen in GG's office in the first place. Joe rose to his feet and said to one of the police officers, "When authorities at the interior ministry demand to be shown a proof of competence from a juju-man before been issued a license to practice as a native doctor, they should not panic at what may appear. Mr. Gordonson asked me a few moments ago to demonstrate proof of why I should be licensed to practice as a native doctor; and the snake seen under his desk was the simplest proof I could demonstrate as a proof of such competence. Could you now request him to come and issue my license so that I may go back to my village?"

Upon hearing the explanation of events directly from Joe, the policeman relayed the message to his colleagues and to the curious crowd that the snake spotted in GG's office was the result of a demonstration of black magic. As such, the crowd and the police squad should disperse at once.

Mr. Gordonson could not believe his ears. He could not comprehend that what he had jokingly requested from his client could result in such a chaotic situation. Trembling in disbelief, GG entered his office and promptly signed and stamped the authorized official license with the interior ministry's insignia, bearing the name of Joe Blackee, to indefinitely practice as a native doctor in the Republic of Liberia.

As GG signed the certificate, he ordered an immediate refund of the full amount earlier offered by Joe as the traditional license fee. In an angry tone of voice he said to Joe, "Don't ever come to my office again; your license is valid for life."

And from that very moment, Joe officially became a fully fledged native doctor.

EIGHTEEN

Strange events often herald the beginning of a new era. And a new era had indeed begun in Freeman Town; the people had never seen anything of its kind.

A stranger in Freeman Town had now transformed himself into a recognized, miracle-working juju-man in their midst. News spread like wildfire in and around the Oil Palm Plantations Company of the emergence of a new powerful native doctor called Joe Blackee. Soon, strangers from near and far began to arrive in Freeman Town, staying at the home of Joe's loyal friend, Ngumbu.

Ngumbu at once reflected on his own personal past experiences of how the notion of befriending unknown strangers, including those in police uniforms, could be disastrous.

Ngumbu therefore, decided to share these personal experiences with Joe so as to avoid similar consequences he had personally endured during his youthful year in his village of origin.

Observing the frequent arrival of unknown strangers in his own compound one morning, Ngumbu rose to his feet and asked whether Joe personally knew the people who were now flooding into Freeman Town of which Joe replied in the negative. At this stage Ngumbu decided to share his past personal experiences with his friend for the first time.

And thus he began:

"I was my parents' only surviving child. My mother died twenty-seven years ago, long before I left Nyandemoh-Lahun, and my father remained my only close friend left on Earth. As time went by, my father fell seriously ill. I tried my best to find a cure for his illness, but to no avail. So late one night, he ordered me to sit by his bedside. In a sad tone, my father told me that he was about to die that very night and that I should listen carefully to what he was about to say."

"He warned me of three things never to do in my life. First, I should never reveal my innermost secrets to a strange woman. Second, I should never befriend a very desperate poor man. And third, I should never trust any man who wears a uniform. 'You may bury my bones, but always keep my words,' my father finally concluded."

"Curiosity soon filled my heart. I asked my father to clearly explain to me why I shouldn't do these three things, but before he could utter a word, death suddenly overtook him. "

"For many weeks after his burial, I kept wondering about the true meanings of my father's last words. In my anguish to find a clue, I decided to go counter to my father's advice. It was not too long before I fell in love with a neighbor's daughter, a beautiful young lady; she moved in to live with me in the same house that I had shared with my father prior to his death. Our love grew from day to day."

"And one day, I saw an old man sweating profusely under a pile of fuel wood. I asked him why he was carrying such a big pile of wood. He told me that cutting and selling fuel wood was his only means of livelihood, so he was carrying the wood to the open market to sell so that he could buy food. I politely asked him to put the wood in my yard, which he did."

"I then came to an agreement with him that if he supplied my household with fuel wood on a regular basis, I would pay him on a weekly basis as well as provide him with food on a daily basis. The woodcutter readily agreed and became a virtual member of my household."

"Next to my house lived a police sergeant. I had never befriended even though he lived right next door. One evening, while returning home from my rice farm, I found him looking for a bunch of bananas to buy, as he was hungry. I politely invited him to my house to share a meal with me and my partner. From that moment on, we became so friendly that my partner used to refer to us as twins."

"In spite of my alliance with each of these three individuals, which was obviously in contravention of my late father's advice, the real meaning of his words remained an enigma to me. Then one day, I left the house early in the morning and went to a little village not far from our town. There, I purchased a sheep. I took the animal to the graveside of my father and slaughtered it to his memory. I invoked his spirit to reveal to me the true meaning of his last words before his death."

"As I completed the traditional rituals, I buried the dead animal by my father's graveside: I rubbed the blood of the animal on my clothes and then made my way back home, where I arrived late that evening. When I got home, I went straight into the kitchen and changed my clothes. I then asked my partner to prepare me hot water to have my evening bath, which she did. I then lied to my partner that I had been involved in a fight with a stranger who was attempting to steal our rice in the barn and in the process I killed him. I showed her the blood-stained clothes and told her to hide them, which she did. I warned her never to tell anyone as long as she lived, and she solemnly vowed upon Sande secret society never to reveal the secret to anyone."

"Many weeks went by, and our trust in each other was as solid as ever, but then one evening something terrible happened."

"I called the police sergeant to join us for our evening meal. His sister was visiting him at the time, and I asked him to bring her along. As the guests arrived, my partner became suspicious that I was in love with the sergeant's sister. She became so jealous that while bringing the food to the dining table, she dropped the entire contents of the meal on the floor. She then ran out of the living room to the kitchen. I followed her there and gave her two light slaps on both sides of her face."

"At that point, she rushed into the corner of the kitchen and unearthed the blood-stained clothes she had hidden. In a loud voice, she cried, out saying: 'Do you want to kill me in the same way you killed and buried a man on our farm?' Upon hearing her voice, the police sergeant walked over to my partner and requested her to repeat what she had just said. She gave the blood-stained shirt and shorts to my police friend and repeated her original accusation."

"Without further comment, the police sergeant handcuffed me and was just about to take me to the police station when the poor woodcutter arrived with another pile of wood. Seeing me in handcuffs and about to be led away, the poor woodcutter pleaded with the police sergeant: not for my release, but for me to be given the chance to pay him for the pile of wood he had supplied over the past week. 'If you take this man away now, he is never going to return here to pay for the wood I've supplied him. I know very well that people who commit murder are bound to face the death penalty."

"As the woodcutter pleaded, the police sergeant led me back into my bedroom, where I got hold of the money to pay him in full before he whisked me away."

"At the police station, I was asked whether I had a lawyer to represent me in court. Just then, I remembered what our primary school teacher used to tell us during school days: "Fools make lawyers rich." Because I wasn't such a fool, I simply told the police that I was going to be my own lawyer. I was then given the opportunity to tell my version of the story. I was able to give a full explanation of the issue."

"It was then that I began to understand the true reason why my father had warned me on his deathbed never to trust and befriend any of these individuals in life. After I had told my story, the police escorted me to the spot where I had killed and buried the sheep. Luckily, the decayed body of the sheep was still intact in the pit where it was buried."

"The homicide squad unearthed the decayed animal's remains, which, coupled with the fact that no one had been reported missing in the community prior to that event, clearly showed that my partner's accusation was false. I was told that I was innocent, and I was released from further detention that same night. At that point, I bade farewell to my partner, the woodcutter, and the police sergeant for the last time."

"Since then, I promised myself never to befriend any of these three types of people again for the rest of my natural life. I decided to be my own best friend, until you came along. I wouldn't like you to fall into a similar trap, so please keep away from the police commander, or anyone else who wears a uniform."

As Ngumbu related his previous life experiences to his friend, Joe informed him that the police commander's third wife had not conceived since their marriage a couple of years ago and had therefore come to him for help. This was acceptable to Ngumbu.

That evening, the police commander brought his wife to Joe and left her there to commence the fertility treatment. But before he could leave, Joe warned him in the presence of his loyal friend that while the woman was undergoing treatment, there should be no bedroom contact between the husband and wife until the treatment period was over, which the couple accepted.

Barely four months into the treatments, however, the woman began to put on weight. In the eighth month, the commander was obliged to take his wife back home, as it was obvious that she was heavily pregnant. Whether the conception occurred prior to or after the treatments remained a mystery.

A month later, a bouncing baby boy was born and was subsequently named Wanda. A few days after the baby was born, the police commander confronted Joe about the issue. He simply said, "I do not manufacture babies: you came to me to treat your wife to conceive, and my job had been done. It is now your duty to ask your wife how she became pregnant."

To protect his reputation, the police commander paid Joe the agreed treatment fee of three hundred dollars, a bag of rice, and a lamb. And there ended the issue of the mysterious pregnancy of the police commander's junior wife in Freeman Town.

NINETEEN

Miracles attract public attention and bring great crowds in traditional West African societies. In the case of Joe's transformation from aggrieved retired laborer to juju-man, this was no exception. Joe's successful treatment of the police commander's wife became a turning point in his newly acquired profession. People began to flock to Freeman Town from near and far. While some came there to solve their social, economic, and personal problems, others came there mainly to destroy their enemies. Every hour of the day, Joe's landlord's yard was full of people and livestock.

This continued unabated for two years. Now that money flowed into his coffers, going hungry was a distant memory. Ngumbu was able to abandon his subsistence farming in order to become Joe's full-time middleman. It was no longer necessary for either of them to do manual work.

While the success of Joe's newly acquired juju skills greatly benefited many people in and around the oil palm plantations, it effectively deprived others of their livelihood. One such persons was the Right Reverend Jeremiah, the founder of the African Apostolic Church, in close proximity to the Oil Palm Plantations Company.

Reverend Jeremiah was a well-known and talented conservative evangelical preacher who had surrounded himself with a group of young women, with the understanding that they would serve not only in spiritual capacities—such as open-air preachers and in the choir—but to also serve as domestic assistants to his wife.

The flamboyant reverend then introduced an infamous "midnight vigil" held every Wednesday. Members of the congregation soon noticed something suspicious about the Rev. Jeremiah. The male church members of the congregation, in particular, raised serious concerns about the reverend's habit of disappearing from the church premises shortly after midnight service, only reappearing late the next morning. Most female church members, on the other hand, expressed the view that the reverend was their man of God, sent to convert sinners and lead mankind to salvation.

The reverend's wife became convinced that she had to keep an eye on her husband's movements. It came to a breaking point one evening when jealousy erupted among female members of the congregation over Reverend Jeremiah, who recognized one of his inner spiritual weaknesses. To avoid further embarrassment, Reverend Jeremiah openly told his congregation during the midnight service that "in this religious ministry, no one is perfect!"

Prior to the emergence of "the new deliverer" in Freeman Town, Rev. Jeremiah's compound, commonly referred to as the Apostolic Faith Home, had always been filled with people from all walks of life. As people became aware of Joe's juju-assisted ability to heal various ailments in the community, however, the reverend's congregation began to dwindle significantly. This led to a sharp reduction in weekly church revenue, as many church members failed to attend church or to pay their dues. The situation reached its lowest point one Sunday when the Rev. Jeremiah's senior pastor defected to become an assistant to the new juju-man in Freeman Town. Many of the church's previously loyal worshipers began to defect to Freeman Town as well.

To instill confidence in his few remaining loyal followers, Rev. Jeremiah delivered a powerful sermon to a small gathering of his congregation one Sunday morning, in which he said, "Lucifer had declared war on the Church of God, and unless something was done to destroy the devil, the Church of God was doomed to crumble."

In the days that followed, the reverend visited several villages in and around the plantations to recruit new converts, inviting them to join the African Apostolic Church and to be baptized in the name of Jesus for the salvation of their souls. The reverend gained at least ten new followers. The following Sunday morning, he told his small group of converts to accompany him to Freeman Town for an open-air preaching venture.

The group arrived in Freeman Town with small wooden crosses in their hands and began singing inflammatory songs against Joe Blackee. The reverend then urged his followers to continue the preaching event on a daily basis until the juju-man was finally driven out of the periphery of the plantations company. The open-air preaching continued unabated for seven unbroken days. During this period, the people of Freeman Town couldn't enjoy their morning sleep, nor their afternoon nap.

On the morning of the seventh day, a larger crowd of converts, headed by Reverend Jeremiah, converged on the premises of Joe's landlord, Ngumbu. This time, Joe could not take any more of their nonsense. He went to his room and dressed himself in the same way he had done when he went to Lopolu nearly two years earlier: black shorts and a black T-shirt, topped with a black hat decorated with cowry shells. Holding the tail of a white horse with one hand, he held a live white chicken with the other.

Joe slowly walked toward the reverend. The noise of the preaching ceased as the followers of the apostolic faith held their breath. They thought the flamboyant juju-man had come to repent in order to appease their man of God. Joe stood in front of the reverend without saying a word to him. He then whispered into both ears of the chicken and placed it at the feet of Reverend Jeremiah. Joe gestured as if he were about to kneel before the preacher. Instead, he stood up and said in a loud voice: "Let everyone pay attention to what is about to happen here."

The white chicken flew up twelve feet above the ground and came down on its neck, dead. As the bewildered crowd watched, a horde of maggots emerged from nowhere and covered the chicken. Its white feathers turned black, as if it had been dead for weeks. Joe stood up again and pointed his right index finger at the rotten chicken and said, "Enough of your malicious preaching: you people have tormented my clients and my neighbors in Freeman Town for seven straight days now. You have called me names that I don't deserve. Let this be a warning to you. Starting today, if I hear one more word of your malicious preaching, anyone involved will die in the same way in which that chicken has died. There will be no need for a burial, as the maggots will take care of your corpses."

Each of the reverend's preachers fled Freeman Town as quickly as possible. The failed preaching venture was the reverend's last glimmer of hope to dislodge his avowed enemy from Freeman Town. *The Oracle* carried a special article in its editorial the next morning: "The Miraculous Juju-man of Freeman Town Ruins the Church of the Apostolic Faith: The Church Crumbles."

TWENTY

Productivity naturally declines with age. As Joe's popularity reached its climax in Freeman Town, his health began to decline rapidly. To everyone's astonishment, Joe again began to behave strangely, just as when he first moved to Freeman Town some years earlier. At times, mostly in the middle of the day, he would hallucinate, and people could hear him speaking in languages not spoken by anyone in Freeman Town. Some people maintained that the adverse effects of Joe's powerful juju had taken a toll on him. Others concluded that Joe was now in the spiritual domain and was therefore speaking to the dead.

Joe also began to have strange dreams at night, which he told his loyal friend about the following mornings. These dreams were of an extraordinary nature, as they reflected Joe's real life. These often unpredictable dreams were followed by mysterious natural events in Freeman Town.

On one occasion, the inhabitants of Freeman Town were awakened early one morning by a frightening outburst of shouting from one of Joe's female patients. The woman had opened the front door while going outside to attend to nature. As she stepped over the door step, she stepped on a slow-moving object. She jumped out of her skin: a large king cobra was slowly crawling out of the house. She realized that for some reason the snake had not bitten her. As men and boys hastened to grab weapons to kill the snake, it slithered away into oblivion, just as mysteriously as it had arrived.

That same afternoon, Joe's landlord nearly fainted when he spotted a strange, multicolored chameleon crawling out of his veranda. As he attempted to kill the creature, it also vanished without a trace. That evening, a black raven flew out of Joe's bedroom. As children ran to kill the bird for their evening meal, it too flew away and disappeared into the darkness.

These events became a source of serious concern, especially for the town chief and his councilmen. Throughout the history of their settlement, nothing of this nature had ever occurred in the same day. Three of the senior elders who had observed the mysterious events stood under a mango tree facing Joe's window. They began a lengthy discussion that started quietly but had soon developed into a heated argument among themselves. They began to exchange personal views on the events of the day. One of them said loudly, "In times like these, it is Joe Blackee who should be guiding us."

This statement was acknowledged by another elder, who calmly said, "But we hardly see him these days. He does not even associate himself with anyone, let alone interpret enigmatic events like these."

The third elder scratched his head several times. And as he stood with arms akimbo, he said to his bewildered colleagues, "The appearance of a cobra, chameleon, or black raven in a village at any time has always been considered to be a bad omen!"

The three elders then became speechless. The silence was finally broken by one of them, who said, "When things like this happened in Freeman Town in ancient days, our elders said it heralded an accidental death of a young person, or the natural death of a prominent member of the community." Another elder acknowledged this, but went on to say (to the distaste of his colleagues), "In that case, it could either be the death of one of us, or that of the juju-man." Another elder put an end to the discussion: "We have to wait and see what happens in the coming days." Each of the elders then set off in different directions.

Joe became worried one night when, half dreaming and half hallucinating, he saw the ghosts of seven men from Lopolu, headed by their chief juju-man, Gotola. Although Joe was aware that these men had died long ago, following the seizure of their juju paraphernalia, they demanded the return of their items. The ghost of Gotola said to Joe, "We have come to take our juju from you back to Lopolu. This has to be done without delay."

Following this, Joe had another dream in which he saw a terrifying monster, the likes of which he had never seen in his conscious life. The creature was so fearful and so violent that it shook the universe and swallowed both the sun and the moon. There was total darkness upon the surface of the Earth. In the ensuing pandemonium, Joe saw himself carried away by the force of a mighty tide, and there was no one to come to his rescue. As Joe awoke in a panic, he asked himself, "What could all these events mean? Could this be the end of mankind, or that of my own life?"

The next morning, Joe approached Ngumbu and said to him, "Very soon a terrible thing is going to happen in this village!" Joe did not elaborate further, so Ngumbu did not know if Joe meant himself, Ngumbu, or someone else in the community.

"Could we make sacrifices to preclude such an event?" he asked.

"No, there is no antidote for this. Whatever is ordained by the Almighty God cannot be prevented by an offer of sacrifice!"

"Then we should be ready for the inevitable consequences," remarked Ngumbu.

At noon that same day, Joe emerged from his room perspiring profusely. This time he was fully dressed in his traditional juju regalia: black shorts, black T-shirt, and a black hat, nicely decorated with cowry shells. In his right hand, he held his familiar symbol of cultural authority, the white horsetail. Waving and hitting the object over both shoulders, he went round the compound four times, followed by a ritual hitting of the ground with the horsetail.

Observing the proceedings from his hammock, Ngumbu thought his friend was performing a sacred ritual to circumvent the impending catastrophe he had predicted that morning. This caused him to remark that "events considered bad in dreams could at times turn out to be the opposite!"

TWENTY-ONE

Warning comes before a fall. From all indications, dreams warn people of what is to befall them in life. Seven years had now passed since the advent of Joe's juju in Freeman Town. One evening, the sky was clearer than usual and the moon was shining to its fullest. This attracted many of the children of Freeman Town to gather in their usual spot at the center of the village to play under the brightness of the full moon.

In the midst of their play, the moonlight began to fade away and the sky became darker. The elders, who had observed the change of events, began chatting among themselves and agreed that it was a total eclipse of the moon. "It occurs once in a generation," one elder remarked.

Beating the back of an empty tortoise shell, the town crier summoned the young men and women of Freeman Town to join the children in the center of the village to sing and beg the eclipse to let the moon shine again. Obeying the town crier's call, the townspeople chanted traditional songs long into the night. The chanting stopped only when the eclipse subsided and the bright light of the moon reappeared.

With the frightening memories of his dream about the monster fresh in his mind, coupled with the eclipse, Joe became more and more worried. To him, the appearance of an eclipse of the moon had always been a symbol of death. Even during his youth in his native village, an eclipse heralded the death of a senior elder or a nobleman in the community. On this particular occasion, Joe feared it could be the symbol of his own death.

Joe could not sleep that night, as he was in agony. He didn't let his friend know, since he thought he could manage his pain, just as any man who underwent the rituals of Poro initiation did. The severity of the pain spread to every part of his body.

The following morning, Joe looked pale and felt weak. As he emerged from his room, he walked slowly toward the thatched-roof bathroom to ease himself after a sleepless night. Walking back to the house, Joe stopped and turned his face to look in the direction of the sun. Pointing his right index finger toward his hometown in the northeast of Liberia, Joe again reflected on the bitter memories of his early life. He loudly repeated the name of his beloved village four times, saying:

"Nyandemoh-Lahun!"

"Nyandemoh-Lahun!"

"Nyandemoh-Lahun!"

"Nyandemoh-Lahun!"

Joe then walked slowly into his bedroom. Speaking to himself in a low voice, he said, "What a man acquires in life by intimidation and deception, cannot by virtue be inherited after his demise, even by his offspring!" He knew that his ill-gotten juju paraphernalia could not be inherited or passed down, either to his sons or to his friend Ngumbu.

As Joe's illness worsened, there was another total eclipse of the moon the following evening, in which young people and children performed similar rituals befitting the occasion until the moon reappeared. On the morning following the second eclipse, Joe failed to wake up.

Prior to his illness, Joe had always been the first to wake up in the morning to attend his patients and the last in Freeman Town to go to bed at the end of the day. As the sun rose this day, Ngumbu came out of his bedroom and tiptoed to Joe's door. He knocked gently on the door but got no answer. He then loudly called his dear friend's birth name four times:

"Fatoma!"

"Fatoma!"

"Fatoma!"

"Fatomaaaaaaaaaaa!"

Still, there was no response. Ngumbu then forced the door open and entered the room. As he entered Joe's bedroom, Ngumbu observed that Joe had died sometime that night or in the early morning hours. Ngumbu also observed that Joe's juju paraphernalia had also vanished during the same time.

By midday, Ngumbu, along with the elders of Freeman Town, organized a proper burial ceremony for Joe, which was attended by thousands of well-wishers in and around the Oil Palm Plantations Company. As a mark of respect to a long-serving laborer of the company, the general manager, Mr. J. Volgan Barnett, who had originally written to Joe of his enforced retirement, sent a hearse and a driver to take the mortal remains of his former employee for burial. He himself never attended the ceremonies.

In respect for his role as a native doctor, Joe was buried in his simple juju traditional regalia: black shorts, black T-shirt, and a hat decorated with cowry shells. He was wrapped in a white burial garment. No shoes were put on his feet, in accordance with his juju orientation. As tradition dictated, Joe's remains were not placed in a coffin or casket.

To everyone's surprise, Reverend Jeremiah, accompanied by a group of worshipers from his African Church of the Apostolic Faith, arrived in Freeman Town not long after the burial of his avowed enemy. He came with a choir that was specially organized for Joe Blackee's funeral ceremonies.

Reverend Jeremiah commenced the service by singing three verses of one of his most beloved hymns, "The Band of Saints on High," which was echoed by the congregation:

The band of saints on high!

> *Around the glorious throne!*
> *Alleluia they sweetly cry!*
> *In joy they gladly roam!*
>
> *The band of saints on high!*
> *Around the glorious throne!*
> *Alleluia they sweetly cry!*
> *Their souls are satisfied!*
>
> *The band of saints on high!*
> *In strife they won the crown!*
> *Oh! Struggle hard as they did fight!*
> *You too may wear the crown!*

The third verse of the hymn was repeated several times by the reverend and echoed by the congregation. When he knew that the hymn had taken its full effect on the congregation, Reverend Jeremiah ended the hymn by saying, "Amen," three times. The congregation as one echoed his powerful voice, saying, "Amen."

Then the reverend took out a white handkerchief from the side pocket of his vestment and twice wiped his face. He stood with his head bowed. He opened the Holy Bible but did not read from it. Instead, he closed the Bible, gently placed it on the little makeshift table before him, and once again said, "Amen!" The awaiting congregation again thunderously echoed his powerful amen. In a brief tribute to his one-time enemy, Reverend Jeremiah described Joe as "a man with great supernatural prowess in the community. A man without an equal who dominated the lives of so many people in and around the Oil Palm Plantations Company and beyond, for a memorable period."

The reverend concluded his tribute by saying, "In spite of all our spiritual and cultural differences in life, and even though Joe defeated me in life, I have now defeated him in death: I've forgiven him from this day and fervently pray for his soul to rest in the mercy of God Almighty. Let's say 'Amen!'"

And the congregation in chorus said, "Amen."

In honor of Joe's dedicated service to the community, prior to his burial in Freeman Town, seven cannons were fired at midday on the orders of the township commissioner. In addition, a cow, seven sheep, nine goats, and hundreds of chickens were slaughtered at Joe Blackee's graveside to commemorate the passing away of one of Freeman Town's greatest citizens but also one of the plantation's most venerated laborers.

Following the burial ceremonies earlier that afternoon, Joe's friend, Ngumbu, placed a specially designed epithet over the grave of his departed brother, friend, and fallen hero, which read:

"HERE MARKS THE FINAL RESTING PLACE OF JOE BLACKEE, THE GREATEST JUJU-MAN IN FREEMAN TOWN'S HISTORY."

ABOUT THE AUTHOR

The author is a product of the Demographic Unit of the University of Liberia and Sir David Owens Population Center in the United Kingdom. He holds a doctoral degree in social anthropology; a master's degree in economic and social studies from the University of Wales; a postgraduate certificate in post compulsory education and training (PGCE/PCET) from Cardiff School of Social Sciences, Cardiff University; and a higher diploma in psychology and criminology in the community. He is also a mental health first aider and a trained transactional analyst, specializing in stress management.

The author was for many years, a school teacher at the Samuel Grimes Memorial Institute in Kakata City, rural Liberia, before becoming a senior statistician and assistant director for research and statistics at the then Liberia Ministry of Rural Development in Monrovia from 1980-1989. He was an associate tutor at the Cardiff School of Social Sciences from 2009-2011. He co-authored the research findings into the mental state of refugees and asylum seekers in Wales for the Welsh Refugee Council, entitled Healthy Minds at Work, published in 2009. He has served in various capacities at the Welsh Refugee Council, including inclusion officer for refugee education and training (2010-2011), policy and research officer (2011-2012), quality information officer (2012), and subsequently advice case worker (2012-2013).

The author also served as volunteer international welfare officer for the British Red Cross Society in Cardiff from 2000–2007, where he assisted with the tracing and delivery of messages to people separated by civil conflicts and natural disasters. He simultaneously served as volunteer administrative assistant with Oxfam Wales headquarters in Cardiff from 2000–2007, where, among other administrative duties, he helped take phone calls from potential donors and the general public in times of natural disasters, including the catastrophic 2004 Indian Ocean tsunami.

The author is now a professional freelance journalist and independent writer in Cardiff City, Wales, United Kingdom.